THE CONFESSION OF O.J. SIMPSON

A WORK OF FICTION

THE CONFESSION OF O.J. SIMPSON

A WORK OF FICTION

DAVID BENDER

BERKLEY BOOKS, NEW YORK

THE CONFESSION OF O. J. SIMPSON: A WORK OF FICTION

A Berkley Book / published by arrangement with the author.

First edition: August 1997

Copyright © 1997 by David Bender

The Putnam Berkley World Wide Web site address is
http://www.berkley.com

ISBN: 0-425-16205-2

BERKLEY®
Berkley Books are published by The Berkley Publishing Group,
200 Madison Avenue, New York, New York 10016,
a member of Penguin Putnam Inc.
BERKLEY and the ''B'' design are trademarks belonging to
Berkley Publishing Corporation.

PRINTED IN THE UNITED STATES OF AMERICA

10   9   8   7   6   5   4   3   2   1

*To my mother, whose love gives me
wings and whose confidence allows me to soar.*

And for my mowgli.

Acknowledgments

Every book has a life of its own. This one is no exception. Although it is entirely the product of my own imagination, it never would have existed outside that crowded and confused place were it not for the unbelievable efforts of two extraordinary people: my editor, Nanscy Neiman-Legette, and my agent, Al Lowman. Each of them believed in this book from the start. Their passion, determination, kindness, patience and general joies du libres are the reasons this novel came into being. Al, you are my knight. Nanscy, you are the patron saint every writer should be blessed with. I am profoundly grateful to you both, now and forever.

I also need to express my gratitude to David Crosby, my writing partner on a book which remains unfinished because I took time away from it to write this novel. His graciousness in deferring our work together so I could follow this flight of fancy to its destination is entirely in character for him. He is one of the most generous, compassionate, and loving human beings I've ever known, let alone been lucky enough to call my friend.

For his belief in me as a writer, his confidence in me as a contributor, and his faith in me as a friend, I want to give special thanks to John Kennedy.

Different people played crucial parts in helping me finish

Acknowledgments

this book. For his counsel and support during the writing, I am very grateful to my friend of almost twenty-eight years (gulp), Steven Pressman. For their lifelong love and friendship (never more valuable than when I labored over this manuscript), my deepest thanks to Stan and Karen Baratta. Marianne Williamson offered her prayers and inspiration, and for that I am particularly grateful.

Special credit and appreciation also go to Jaime Capone, without whom the last half of this book could not have been finished; to Elaine Creos-Piechowski, for her tireless efforts and constant good cheer, even in the face of yet another trip to the airport; to Dean Williamson, B. G. Dilworth, Charlotte Patton and Maggie Lang from Authors' and Artists' Agency for all their work on behalf of this book and their kindness to its author; to Phil Sutfin, for giving me consistent shelter from the New York storm; to John Detch, for his computer wizardry; and to Damien Craft, for his healing talent as a massage therapist.

I've stood on many other shoulders to reach this point. You know who you are. So do I. And I thank you all.

Author's note to the reader

I hadn't planned on writing this book. In fact, I was at my computer in the middle of another book—not a novel—when the idea for *The Confession of O. J. Simpson: A Work of Fiction* first came to me. At the time, it was very much an uninvited intruder in my life.

But the idea wouldn't go away. Fred Goldman had just made a very public offer to give back the millions of dollars awarded to him by a civil jury which held Simpson liable for the death of his son. All Goldman said he wanted in return was the truth. What had really happened on June 12, 1994? It wouldn't bring back his son, but it would give him the peace of mind that no amount of money could buy.

What if O. J. Simpson accepted Goldman's challenge? What would happen then?

When Goldman issued his challenge to Simpson, I started thinking about the constitutional protection afforded anyone who has been tried and found not guilty of committing a particular crime. The principle of ''double jeopardy'' protects someone from ever being tried again for that same crime. (Simpson's civil trial was not governed by this principle as there were no criminal penalties involved.) Given his immunity from future criminal prosecution, Simpson could, if he chose, tell the world anything he wanted about his involvement in the murders. Difficult as it might be for some to believe, if he actually *did* confess tomorrow, the only criminal charges he might conceivably face would be for perjury, based on his testimony in the civil trial.

This was the premise which led me to write this book. It's a story that seemed to will itself into being written. Like everyone else, I was hoping for a sense of closure after the criminal and civil trials. But, this was not to be. The two juries issued conflicting verdicts. I found this absence of resolution impossible to accept. With *The Confession of O. J. Simpson: A Work of Fiction,* I've tried to use fiction to make the bizarre reality of the Simpson case more comprehensible. If I've done it right, perhaps it will provide some measure of resolution to those who continue to obsess about this case. Perhaps not.

I have never met nor even seen O. J. Simpson. Nor do I have any inside knowledge about his life or the events surrounding the murder trials.

My closest connection to him came when I looked out the window of my Santa Monica apartment in the late afternoon of June 17, 1994, and saw a swarm of helicopters circling overhead in what appeared to be a scene from *Apocalypse Now*. In fact, they were waiting for Al Cowlings's Bronco which, at that moment, was still a few miles away, heading north on the 405 Freeway. I knew its precise location because, like everyone else in America, I was watching the infamous ''slow-speed'' chase as it unfolded on television. The helicopters buzzing around my neighborhood were actually in a holding pattern over Nicole Brown's condominium on Bundy Drive. As it happened, the

"Crime of the Century" had been committed just a mile away from my apartment.

Presumably the helicopters were hovering over Bundy because it was assumed Simpson would do what the guilty are always *supposed* to do: return to the scene of the crime. But as everyone now knows, the Bronco never made it to Bundy that day. Instead, Simpson returned to Rockingham, where a welcome-home party had been thoughtfully arranged by a SWAT team from the Los Angeles Police Department. It wouldn't be the last time O. J. Simpson would confound the expectations of those who thought they understood him or this case.

I followed the criminal trial closely. Working from home, I often keep the television on during the day. This provided me with constant exposure to what became the most-watched program in the history of daytime television: a uniquely American drama known as the "Simpson Case." For over a year—from jury selection through the verdict—I'm not ashamed to admit I, along with millions of others, was transfixed by the criminal case.

There are very few moments in the life of a nation when time stops, when our collective breath is held and we all remember where we were and exactly what we were doing. President Kennedy's assassination, the moon landing, the Challenger explosion, and, like it or not, the Bronco chase and the not-guilty verdict, were such moments.

When the criminal verdict was read, saturation television coverage created a kind of "echo chamber" effect. That effect was observed (and intensified) as we watched the faces of Americans simultaneously reacting to the verdict. Jubilant blacks and stunned whites seemed to be the pattern. Those people who were appalled by the verdict were made even angrier by the joyous reactions they were witnessing, largely among African-Americans. Those who believed that justice—finally—had been delivered to a black man in America, were equally enraged that his "victory" was now being decried as a blatant example of *injustice*.

In my judgment—a judgment shared by many others who have written about the Simpson case—this was never about race at all. It was and remains a story about America's obsession with celebrity over substance—and virtually everything else. The enduring tragedy is that instead of recognizing this, we seem to have further compounded it. Even the minor players in the Simpson saga have been elevated to the level of prominence once reserved for saints and Supreme Court justices.

O. J. Simpson maintains his innocence to this day and he has a jury's unanimous support for his claim. Fred Goldman and the Brown family are equally adamant that Simpson is a murderer who has gone free and *they* can point to the unanimous decision of a jury which held him liable for the killings. The nation remains a mirror of this uncertainty, with people still remarkably passionate on both sides of the question. And although racial lines have always been sharply drawn around this case, it's clear they neither predict nor define a person's belief about what really happened. My seventy-nine-year-old Jewish mother, for example, still doesn't believe the police have ever looked for the real killer or killers.

Author's Note to the Reader

Several of the premises on which *The Confession of O. J. Simpson: A Work of Fiction* is based are patently false. For example, Mrs. Eunice Simpson is, happily, still very much alive. And Marcus Allen did not return from the Cayman Islands until the week *after* the Bronco chase and Simpson's subsequent arrest. To my knowledge, Ron Goldman never had a private encounter with O. J. Simpson, and I am certainly not aware of the existence of any audio tapes of conversations between O. J. and Nicole (with the exception of her widely replayed distress call to 911, which can hardly be called a conversation).

Most important, two *real* people were brutally murdered on June 12, 1994. Their names are Ronald Goldman and Nicole Brown. I've learned much about them in the process of writing this novel.

Here's what I've come to know about them. Nicole was in an abusive relationship for her entire adult life and managed to get out of it—in no small part for the sake of the children she loved. Then she was murdered. Ron had the unlimited dreams of a young man who was deeply loved by his family and friends. He died a hero, trying to save the life of a friend. I believe the Goldman family's indefatigable search for justice has been the one ennobling lesson of the entire public drama.

I also have particular empathy for those who have lost a loved one violently. Someone I loved very much was murdered and part of me died that day, too. That kind of sudden, wrenching loss is almost impossible to comprehend right away. The mind struggles to understand the truth, but can't process it. Precisely because it *is* so hard to derive any meaning from a tragedy of this magnitude, I hope this novel might provide another way for people to come to terms with the tragic yet surreal events of this case and its aftermath.

It should be emphasized again that this is entirely a work of fiction. I haven't been provided with any facts or insights about the real O. J. Simpson which are not available to the general public. As I said at the beginning, I do not know Simpson, nor have I met anyone else referred to in this book, with two exceptions: President Clinton, whom I've met briefly on a few occasions at political events and Roosevelt Grier, whom I last saw in 1968 when I was a twelve-year-old volunteer on the presidential campaign of Senator Robert F. Kennedy. Indeed, I've avoided all possible contact with anyone who knows Simpson or who might be able to tell me anything that isn't already public knowledge about him or this case. For the record, I am *not* related to Robert "Bobby" Bender, the New York businessman who has been a longtime friend of the real O. J. Simpson. Also, the character of the therapist, Dr. Donald Weiss, is entirely fictitious. He is in no way based on any of the real doctors and therapists who reportedly have treated Simpson at various points in his life.

The following key events in this book are true: Nicole Brown and Ronald Goldman *were* murdered on June 12, 1994; O. J. Simpson and Al Cowlings *did* leave Robert Kardashian's house in Encino on June 17, 1994, culminating in the so-called "slow-speed chase" through Orange County and Los Angeles; O. J. Simpson *was* tried and acquitted on the criminal charges filed against him for those murders; subsequently, Simpson *was* judged to be civilly liable for the deaths of Goldman and Brown

Author's Note to the Reader

and a jury awarded the plaintiffs, including Fred Goldman, a total of $33.5 million in combined punitive and compensatory damages; and Fred Goldman *did* challenge Simpson to publicly confess his guilt in return for which he would waive his share of that judgment.

Except for the above, to my knowledge, none of the events depicted in this novel, or statements made by the characters in it, is true or purports to be true in any way.

David Bender
May 1997

THE CONFESSION OF
O.J. SIMPSON
A WORK OF FICTION

CHAPTER ONE

The phone call that morning came in on my private line.

"This is O.J. Do you remember me?"

I was startled at the sound of his voice. Memories came crashing together. The golf game four—or was it five?—years ago, when I rounded out a foursome after Kardashian had canceled at the last minute; the dinner party at Rockingham where (to O.J.'s considerable amusement) I got into a theological argument, with, of all people, Kato Kaelin (Kato: "How could Jesus have been a Jew if He was the Son of God? God doesn't have a particular religion; that's why he's *God*." O.J.: "Get Kato a collar! Don't mess with Father Kato, Sam, he'll *excommunicate* you!"); the awkward encounter at the Palm Beach airport last winter when I saw him before he saw me and he caught me trying to hail a cab without acknowledging him; both of us pretending that it hadn't happened and him asking for my

1

card ("I need a lawyer who isn't trying to hustle me for business"); me writing down my number, fully expecting that he'd never use it.

I forced myself to concentrate on the phone call.

"Yes, of course I remember you. Where are you?"

"Here. In San Francisco. I'm helping my sisters pack up my mother's place before it's sold."

"I heard about your mother. I'm sorry."

"Thanks, man. She was a great lady. Listen, Sam. I need to talk to you right away."

"Okay, go ahead."

"No, not on the phone. I need to see you. Today."

"O.J., I'm really busy today. I've got a hearing next week. Can it wait?"

"No, it can't. I'm about to say some things—some things to the press—and I need to know how bad it could get."

"What do you mean, 'bad'?"

"If I say something and they say it's different from what I said in court or in my deposition, isn't that perjury?"

"Probably. Yes."

"So, I need to see you, Sam. Before I commit perjury."

In the half hour it took him to get to my house, I replayed the conversation over and over again in my mind. When he arrived, I ushered him quickly upstairs to my office, hoping that none of my neighbors would see him.

I sat down at my desk and motioned him toward the one chair I had for visitors. He ignored my hospitality and got right to the point.

2

A Work of Fiction

"So, what could I get for perjury?"

His question hung in the air like a cloud in front of the sun. Conversely, the room seemed to grow warmer as I got up from my desk, crossed to the bookshelf, and ran my finger across the dark spines of a row of leather-bound reference books until I came to one marked *California Penal Code*.

"C'mon, *man* . . . don't you know this stuff in your head? What am I *doin'* here if you don't know this stuff?"

The voice, its familiar baritone resonating in the small room that served as my home-office, was mocking. By now he'd settled on the arm of the chair, still refusing to sit in it. The chair was normally flush against the wall, but he had picked it up and planted it in the center of the room. This was intended to demonstrate two things, neither of which was lost on me: that he could pick up a heavy leather chair effortlessly and that my office was no longer my own domain.

I kept my back to him and didn't answer, not until I found the volume I was looking for. I returned to my desk and laid the book in front of me, open to the citation for perjury.

Deliberately, in a move I could sense irritated him, I read the citation aloud, in its entirety: "California Penal Code Section 118. Perjury defined. (a) Every person who, having taken an oath that he or she will testify, declare, depose or certify truly before any competent tribunal, officer, or person, in any of the cases in which the oath may by law of the State of California be administered, willfully and contrary to the oath, states as true any material matter which he or she knows to be false, is guilty of perjury."

3

On the last sentence, I didn't look at the text; I looked directly at him and watched him watching me as I said the penalty he'd been impatient to hear: "imprisonment for a period of two, three, or four years."

He didn't flinch. He'd heard worse. The impassive mask he wore through two trials and countless hours of television coverage was equally inscrutable in person.

I didn't speak further, waiting for him to break the silence. The only way I knew my words had registered at all was by watching the movement of his right leg. It was shaking—vibrating—as if it had a life of its own. It reminded me of a film I'd seen as a child that showed a dead chicken still running in circles around a barnyard. I shuddered involuntarily when I realized that the chicken had been *decapitated*. . . .

Abruptly, his leg stopped moving and he spoke. This time his voice was quiet, almost reflective.

"You could do that." He was clearly talking to himself even though I was no more than six feet away.

He was nodding now, the rapid movement of his head having replaced the shaking of his leg.

"Yeah, you could do that. You could handle that. Piece of cake." He was psyching himself up and I was a fly on the wall for his personal pep talk.

"You done that. You've done that already." He seemed to correct his grammar for my benefit. Now he was up off the chair, pacing. Since there was so little room to move around in my office, his circuit was limited to the space between the chair, my desk, and the window opposite the bookshelves.

A Work of Fiction

I remembered the image of him in a blue jumpsuit—the Voyeur-Cam shot, taken from a hovering helicopter, of him being returned to the county lockup every night after court. Now, as he was standing by the window, his fingers drumming on the pane, I had that same sensation of watching something I wasn't supposed to see. During the trial, it had been a guilty pleasure, indulged by millions, but no more significant than a midnight bowl of ice cream.

This was different. This was the claustrophobia that comes from being in a small, closed room with a man who may have brutally killed two people.

It's a sensation you just don't get from television.

"Why don't you sit down and we can go over what we talked about on the phone." I was trying to remain matter-of-fact in my tone, as if this was just another day at the office and he was just another client.

He looked over at me, but still didn't see me, as if he'd heard a sound from somewhere but couldn't be certain where it was coming from.

"O.J.!" I spoke sharply into his middle distance.

"Sure. Right. Let's do it."

He came back over to the chair and sat in it properly, almost formally. He locked eyes with me across the desk and I sensed that I was about to receive "the Treatment", the full force of his attention and intensity that I'd read about but never experienced. I wasn't disappointed.

"Look, man. I've got two kids to support and they want to take away everything I have. This isn't easy for me. If my

5

mother was alive, I still wouldn't do this. I couldn't. But they've left me with no choice.''

He was speaking softly now, almost sotto voce. Because I had to listen carefully to hear him, I was drawn into what he was saying. It was an old trick, but effective.

"Do you know what it's *like*? Do you have any *idea*?''

"No, I don't.'' He wasn't looking for an answer, but I didn't want to go down that road of "poor me" with him. I had no interest in it.

"Damn right you don't! Nobody knows. Nobody can imagine what this is like. I can't fuckin' go to the bathroom without a camera following me.''

He was speaking much louder now and I thought if I was directing this scene, I'd yell "cut," and tell him to keep his voice down if he wanted to play it for sympathy. But I kept quiet.

As if he'd heard me, his tone grew soft again and he was plaintive: "Look, I'm sorry. I don't mean to get mad at you. I'm just worried about my kids. They're all I got left. If I don't do this, I can't take care of them and I'm gonna lose 'em.''

"So, what is it exactly you want *me* to do? You said on the phone you wanted to talk to the press and that you were concerned about criminal liability if anything you said contradicted your sworn testimony. I need you to be very specific with me, O.J., if we're to accomplish anything.''

"I want to confess.''

There it was. A man I barely knew and didn't like had just announced he was a double murderer and that he wanted to confess to the Crime of the Century—in my house. My mind started to wander, pondering the enormous implications of what he'd just said.

"Sam!" He had no patience with my drifting.

"I'm sorry. You caught me off guard. You want to confess to *what* exactly?" I was going to make him say it.

"Shit, Sam. I'm not here to play games. You know what I'm talking about. What I need from you is to walk me through this so it doesn't get any worse than it has to. Like you did about Fuhrman on *Larry King*."

So, *that's* what got him here. That debate with Gerry Spence about whether they could convict Mark Fuhrman for perjury.

"You saw that?"

"For about two minutes. I was flipping channels and I saw you trying to convince Larry that just because that cocksucker Fuhrman said 'nigger' a million times, it didn't mean he'd committed perjury. What did you call it? Role-playing? Shit." He was grinning, trying to flatter me.

"You're going to confess to killing two people, something you swore under oath you didn't do, and you want me to help you avoid a perjury charge? O.J., you're wasting my time and yours. It's an impossible case to win. They'll give you the maximum sentence permitted under law."

The mask was back in place.

"I know that. I can handle that." His tone was even.

"I'm sorry, but I really don't understand. What do you need *me* for, if you've made up your mind to admit that you perjured yourself?"

"That's just it, Sam. I'm not prepared to *admit* that it was

7

perjury. All I'm ready to do is sign a confession and I want an airtight agreement with Goldman to give me back the money. Do you follow me?''

I was beginning to.

''You'll make a statement that you killed . . . them . . . and because of double jeopardy you can't be retried. . . .'' My voice trailed off.

''Now you get it.''

''And this is all about getting Fred Goldman to waive the money you owe him, right? How much is it? Twenty million?''

''More. That bitch of a mother—she hardly *talked* to the kid and she's getting seven and a half million. For what? For *nothing*. Anyway, she's not giving up a dime of her share, so Goldman can only give me back his part; it's thirteen and a half million. I could use it.''

He was studying my reaction as I realized what he wanted me to do.

''But you're committing perjury either way, O.J. If you sign a sworn statement—''

''No, man. That's just the thing. He don't want a sworn statement. He wants *details*. He wants me to tell what happened and pay for putting it in all the newspapers. Then he'll give me back my money. He says nothing about swearing out a statement. See, it's right here.''

He pulled a copy of *Newsweek* out of a black leather case that was resting on the floor beside him and put it in front of me, open to a page titled *Perspectives*. I always read that page.

It featured the most newsworthy or interesting quotes from the previous week. His finger pointed to the name Fred Goldman.

I read the quote:

> *If the person whose name I don't use that murdered my son wants to write out a complete confession and publish it in newspapers around the country, we'll be glad to ignore the judgment.*

"Goldman wants a complete confession. Let's give it to him. Shove it up his ass. You write it up. Did you read that shit about somebody giving him a rifle to kill me? That ugly-ass motherfucker wouldn't know which end of a gun to use. He's such a press whore. I can't believe the media lets him get away with shit like that."

He was repulsive. But there was still something strangely pitiable about him, too. When he talked about his kids, I could almost believe he wasn't acting.

Instead of responding to his diatribe, I took out my legal pad. I wrote *Simpson: Confession* across the top.

"So, let me get this straight. You want me to help you write out a credible, airtight confession?"

He nodded.

"And, on the strength of this, you want a legal document from Fred Goldman waiving his judgment against you?"

"You got it."

"Then you really don't need me, O.J. You need a writer. Isn't Dominick Dunne available?"

He didn't rise to the bait.

"He's not privileged. You are."

"What?"

He spoke to me as if to a child. "You're privileged. Anything I say to you has to remain confidential. Unless you're that bastard Kardashian." He spat the name. "Which I know you're not," he said quickly.

"You've got this all figured out, haven't you?"

"I think so. You'll tell me if I don't."

I stood up. "I'm sorry, O.J. This isn't my kind of job. I just don't think I'm right for it." I put out my hand.

He stood up, too, but instead of shaking my hand, he reached down into his case and pulled out a black leather binder with papers falling out of it, which he placed in front of me on the desk.

"Just read this."

"I don't—"

"Listen, Sam. All I'm askin' is that you read this. If you still don't want to do this for me after that, fine. You walk away, no harm, no foul."

I looked at him for a moment, then shook my head and sat back down in my chair. "What is it?"

"Open it. See for yourself."

It was a mess. All different kinds of papers stuffed into a smallish three-ring binder. Some looked like they belonged— they had holes, at least. Dozens of sheets had been ripped from yellow legal pads. There were many typewritten pages, some of which appeared to be correspondence. And in a clear plastic pocket attached to the inside back cover, I saw a handful of miniature audiocassette tapes—microcassettes.

The page on top was a sheet ripped from a yellow legal pad. It was marked "4/10/92." I read the handwritten scrawl, which was irregular but legible:

She didnt see me. I can't believe that goddamn bitch came right to the window and she didnt see me. She is such a stupid bitch when she's in heat. Those fucking candles were the only light. But I could see her. I saw her kneeling over him on the couch His pants down around his ankles and she was sucking his dick. That bastard should have paid me not her. She's such a whore. I taught her how to give a blowjob. When I met her she woudnt even open her mouth. She was such a daddy's girl.

There was more, but I couldn't focus on it.

"You kept a diary?" I was incredulous.

"Nic did. I used to read it all the time . . . she didn't know it. When I saw some of the stuff she was writing about me, I started keepin' my own notes. . . . It's lots of different things . . . sort of a journal. She was always threatening me, you know? Telling me she'd go to the press with what I'd done to her. I had to be ready to put my side of the story out . . . the *real* truth. I had to protect my reputation."

I'd read that Simpson had orchestrated the strategy of his

11

"Dream Team" during the criminal trial—Cochran, Shapiro, F. Lee Bailey—but I hadn't really believed it. Until now.

"It's my only shot. And it's the only shot my kids have. Don't you see? I have no money. No one will give me a job. My friends have already given me all the help they can afford—and more. That jury was a *joke*. I'll be lucky to keep my kids in shoes, let alone pay for their education."

At the mention of shoes, I found myself staring at his. Reeboks.

"If I go public with this, I can make a fortune. You know it's true, man. The best case is that I can get Goldman to give up the money and you keep me out of jail. At the worst, I do some time, but I can pay Judy and Lou from the book and movie deals and still have enough money left over that I wouldn't ever have to worry. My *kids* wouldn't ever have to worry."

He kept coming back to his kids. I believed him when he said they were all he had left in his life. He was getting to me and he knew it. He smiled. Like he used to smile in those Hertz commercials when he ran through the airport and made it on the plane just in time.

And effective pitchman that he was, he moved to close the sale.

"You're the only one who's ever seen these, Sam. Just you. Not Cochran. Not Baker. Not my sisters. Only you." He was leaning in to me now, talking quickly, excitedly. Not letting me have a chance to think. I took a deep breath and let it out slowly before I spoke.

"All right, O.J. What do you want me to do?"

"Just help me, man."

CHAPTER TWO

Simpson was still staring at me hard, trying to stay locked on me with his eyes, but I didn't return his gaze. I kept my head down and again began leafing through the loose, scattered pages in the notebook. I noticed that many of them were computer-generated pages, and without looking up, I asked him, "What *is* all this?"

With a swift movement that caught me by surprise, he extended his arm completely across the desk and grabbed the journal from me. He was so quick that in the split second it took me to look up, he was already back in his chair, the book open in his lap. He hadn't dropped a single page.

I thought of saying "So, how's the arthritis?"—then remembered that he didn't appreciate a joke made at his expense.

Instead, I just shrugged and said, "I thought you wanted me to read that."

"I do, man. I'm just gonna pick out some stuff. Like, see, here's something."

He read aloud:

3/28/97 I loved it. That fucking putz Goldman thought he was gonna get my Heisman trophy. In his dreams. And you know what's perfect? It's right under his nose. One of my boys, one of my LA County boys, he lives out in the Valley maybe a mile from Goldman's house. And he's got that trophy right on his mantle like he won it himself. I told him he should invite Fraud over for dinner some night to see it and he said Juice, you crack me up.

He looked up at me, grinning. "Isn't that the tits, Sam? Goldman—he calls me 'the murderer.' I call him 'Fraud' 'cuz that's what he is. He's a phony, man. He *loves* his son. Sure and I loved my little baby girl that drowned in my pool—*my* pool—at *my* house—the house he ain't never gonna get now that the mortgage people got it—and you wait, Sam, you wait and see who buys it out of mortgage—anyway, I lost my baby, too, and I was a *man*. I got *on* with my life. But Fraud likes being on television, you know what I'm sayin'? Listen, I *know* this shit, man. I know that he loves bein' the center of all this attention. What's he got without me? If he ever says that somebody else killed his kid, he's got *nothing*. Nobody will *care*. He needs The Juice, Sam. The Juice is all he's got. So fuck *him,* man. He's not gonna get my trophies. Or my money. That's why you gotta help me."

14

A Work of Fiction

I knew O. J. Simpson was a compulsive talker. Everyone knew that by now. But it was still amazing—and disturbing—to watch him verbally spinning out of control, like some errantly thrown football that started off in one direction, then spiraled away from its target as if it had a mind of its own. This was the way O.J. talked. The conversations—they were monologues really—were like creatures he brought to life only to have them run amok, destroying everything in their path. And, as he'd learned to his chagrin in the civil trial, Simpson's living torrent of words could be directed back at him, piranha that could devour their own creator.

But even that painful lesson hadn't stopped him. O.J., now and forever, could not shut up.

I had been attempting to take notes during his diatribe, but I'd written down only one phrase: *L.A. County boys.* I asked him what that meant.

"My *boys,* Sammy. My *brothahs.*" He was grinning again, Cheshire-like.

"The deputies who were guarding me when I was in the lockup? They're my friends, man. They know me. I was with them for four hundred and sixty days and I told every one of them that I'd have them over to my house when I got out, and I did. I played golf with 'em. Took 'em on trips. That's how I met the guy who's holding on to my Heisman. He wasn't actually one of my guards, but he told my friends that he wanted an autograph. So I said sure, but it would cost him—he'd have to take my trophy, too. He 'bout shit, man. But it worked. Nobody knows I even know this guy. And they'll never find him."

He paused to bask in his own cleverness, and I jumped in before he could rev up again.

"Okay, so you've written all this down. Explain to me how you want to use it to get Goldman to waive his judgment against you."

"I told you, Sam. Weren't you *listening*?" He was mildly annoyed, but still patient. He didn't want me jumping off the hook he'd so carefully baited.

"Let me go through it with you again." He was standing up now, moving around the room as he talked. Stopping next to the window, Simpson absentmindedly wrapped the cord from the venetian blinds around his right hand.

"*Fred* Goldman"—he deliberately exaggerated the correct pronunciation to show me that he was trying to be cooperative— "wants a public statement from me. You'll write it up. I'll give it to him and he'll give up his judgment against me like he said he would."

"And you think it isn't perjury because you won't swear to this statement under oath? That's true as far as it goes, O.J., but you swore up and down on the stand that you didn't kill anybody. If you confess now *that's* where you will have perjured yourself." If I hadn't recognized the sound of my own voice, I never would have believed I was having this conversation.

Simpson had his back to me. He was looking at a framed picture on my wall, the venetian-blind cord still wrapped around his hand, trailing him like an appendage. The picture he was looking at was one of me with President Clinton, taken at a reception at the Fairmont Hotel during the reelection campaign.

A Work of Fiction

I'd done a little work during the election, as I always did—just enough to keep my hand in. Not enough to sleep in the Lincoln Bedroom or ride on Air Force One. Enough for a picture.

"That bastard never sent me my picture."

"What?"

Simpson grabbed the picture off the wall and threw it on the floor. It shattered, shards of glass flying across the room. I flinched as he was shouting, "That fucking bastard! I played golf with him. He told me how much he *admired* me. What a huge *fan* he was. And he promised me a picture!"

I'd had enough.

"Get out of here, O.J."

"Sam . . ."

"Who the hell do you think you *are*?" I was angry enough to forget who he was myself. "You *do not* come into my house and throw things around. I want you to leave now. I have no interest in helping you." I was trembling with rage, but my voice was steady.

For a moment he was frozen in place, staring at me, his face anguished. Then he slowly bent down and started picking up pieces of broken glass.

"I'm sorry, man. You're right. Just let me clean this up." His voice was almost inaudible. He was on his hands and knees, looking for the scattered shards.

I came around the desk. "Get up, O.J. I'll do that. Just go, okay?"

He pulled himself up on his knees, big pieces of glass in both hands, and looked up at me. His eyes were empty. "I'm

17

sorry, man. I can't help myself sometimes. People *lie* to me. They hate me now. You don't know ... you don't know what it's like. ..."

I said nothing. I just wanted him out of my house.

He put the fragments of glass in his left hand and reached up to grab my arm with his right, bracing himself against me in order to stand. I helped him up, then noticed there was blood on my shirtsleeve.

"Hey, be careful. You cut yourself."

He was even more apologetic.

"I'm sorry, man. I'm *so* sorry. I messed up your picture, now I messed up your shirt. I'll take care of it. Where do you get your shirts? I'll buy you a dozen of 'em. Just tell me where you get them."

"Don't worry about it, O.J. It's no big deal." For some reason, angry as I was, I couldn't help feeling sorry for him. He was so ... *childlike*. I pulled the wastebasket from under my desk and held it out so that he could put the pieces of glass right into it without cutting himself further.

This small act eased the tension a bit and he asked me for a bandage. I kept some in my drawer, along with tissues. I gave him both and he cleaned the wound. It was a small gash on the index finger of his right hand.

"I'm *always* doin' this to myself." He grinned and looked at me hopefully.

Despite myself, I smiled slightly.

"Look, Sam. I blew it. I'm really sorry. Can we start over? Please?"

I didn't answer him, but I walked back around my desk and sat down. He sat back down in the chair, again facing me.

I was hard. "Look, I haven't got time for this. I have a major case in court next week and this is *not* what I need right now." I looked at my watch. "I'll give you ten more minutes. If you want my help, you're going to have to spell it out. And no more bullshit."

"Thanks, Sam. Thank you. I really mean that."

I picked up my pen and yellow pad and asked him again, "So what you want is for me to draft a confession to two murders that you've already sworn you didn't commit. How is that *not* perjury?"

"It's role playing, Sam. Just like Fuhrman did. Just like *you* said he did on *Larry King*."

"I don't understand. . . ."

"I'll agree to the statement. Hell, I'll even publish it in the newspapers, just like he wants me to. Then I'll say I made the whole thing all up."

Give him this, he was clever. What had Kato called him at the party? *The King of the Manipulators*? I'm sure he meant it as a compliment.

"And you'll have an unbreakable release from Goldman that frees you of any further obligation to him?" It was a rhetorical question. I understood his plan completely now.

"If *you* do it, I know it will be unbreakable." He was feeling slightly more confident with me now, as evidenced by this mild attempt at flattery.

"But even if you get him to release you from the judgment,

19

you'll be hated for the lie," I said. "The public—the media—will take you apart. What good will it do you?"

He looked at me as though I were a little slow. "They hate me *now,* Sam. Shit, I can't even rent a fucking *Hertz* car anymore. I can't do anything about the public. But I *can* take care of my kids if I pull this off. Hell, the money don't even have to go to me. He can sign it over to the trust fund I got set up for the kids."

Good move, Juice, I thought. *You see an opening and run right toward it.*

"So, assuming for the sake of discussion you succeed at doing this, isn't it true that all you've really done is wipe out a debt you never would have been able to pay anyway? I'm sorry to be blunt, O.J., but aren't you broke?"

With his newly bandaged right hand, he reached down and picked up the black notebook, which was still lying on the floor next to where the Clinton photo had landed. He held it in front of him, like an offering.

"Not with this, man. This is the pot of gold and you're my rainbow."

He was winding up again.

"Don't you see, man? I can *publish* this. Not the stuff I had to put in my other book about 'the truth being found in the world of Faye Resnick'—that goddamn *bitch*—this is about what really happened with me and Nicole. If I don't have to pay Goldman, I can keep most of what I make from a book and a movie. And it'll be a lot of money, Sam. *A lot of money.* Fifteen million is what they offered me before to write a book called *I Want to Tell You the Truth.* And you can have twenty-five percent of it, Sam.''

For the second time in less than an hour he offered the journal to me. However, in that brief span, the dynamic between us had drastically changed. This time it was implicitly understood that if I took the black leather notebook from him, it meant I would accept his offer. My eye noticed something on the cover. A tiny drop of blood. It hadn't been there before. Or had it?

CHAPTER THREE

I took the journal from him. It was a smaller version of one of those three-ring binders a college student would use, although like everything Simpson owned (or had *once* owned) it was well made. Black leather-bound, with a zipper around the side that allowed it to close up. Probably Abercrombie & Fitch.

Fumbling in my shirtpocket for my reading glasses, I opened it and tried to decide where to start reading. The problem was it was so jammed full of loose pages, it was difficult to know where to begin.

Simpson remained quietly seated in the chair, studying me as I leafed through the papers on top. His life was now—quite literally—an open book for me to examine. If he still had any doubts about trusting me with it, his expression didn't reveal them. The mask was once again firmly in place.

The Confession of O.J. Simpson

"Take a look at some of those yellow ones," he said, referring to the sheets that had been torn from a yellow legal pad.

All of them were covered with Simpson's unruly scrawl, which made them very difficult to read. I picked up one:

6/22/94 This is not happening. I dont believe this is real. Im real tired all the time maybe I am dreaming this. Shapiro says that the stuff the doctor gave me was strong. No shit. He wants me to write down how I feel. Is that suppose to help me? I feel like shit. When is paula coming? I dont believe I have to stay here. Why not bail? Where am I gonna GO? They have my passport I cant go nowere. What time is it? Fucking Shapiro said they woud not steal my watch. Thats an $8000 rolex Bob. You think Im ever gonna get it back? Bob gets home. Wife and kids. beverly fucking hills. Im sitting here and he goes home every nite. Im by myself. They got everybody out of here for "my protection." Except only one that kid who killed his parents. Erik Mendez. And he talks to me. Like Im his friend. Dont trust Shapiro. He'll sell you out he did that to me. I didnt say nothin to him.

I paused. There was more on the other side. Simpson had been studying my reactions while I was reading.

"Which part was that?" he asked.

"You were in jail, I guess. Just after you were arrested. It's about Shapiro and Erik Menendez."

"Damn if that little faggot kid wasn't right on. He said from

24

day one I should fire Shapiro. He had *that* right. He said he'd sell me out, make a deal to make himself look good. '*Oh Barbara, we played the race card from the bottom of the deck.*' Like he had *nothing* to do with any of it. Where were you for a *year,* Bob? Israel?"

I cut him off before he could get even more offensive.

"What's this?" I held up what appeared to be a letter of some kind. It was typewritten on eight-and-a-half-by-eleven-inch paper, but had been folded into thirds, as if it had been sent in an envelope. There were five pages, stapled together.

"Let me see that."

I handed it to him.

"Oh, this is . . . this is from when I went to the shrink. I don't know if you need to read this."

"Listen, O.J., I don't *need* to read any of it. This was your idea, remember?"

I was testing him.

He looked at me for a long moment and then tossed the letter back across the desk. "Knock yourself out," he said.

I unfolded it. It appeared to be a transcript of some kind. At first I thought it might be an excerpt from a legal deposition, but then I noted the heading: *Donald Weiss, Ph.D. Transcription of Patient Visit, May 4, 1994.*

I began to read.

This is Dr. Donald Weiss. This is a tape recording of a therapy session conducted with my patient, Mr. Orenthal James Simpson. Today's date is May 4, 1994. This tape is made with the full consent of Mr. Simpson and with the understanding that a full

The Confession of O.J. Simpson

transcription will be made available only to him and that this recording will remain in a secured place in my possession. The sum and substance of this session is protected under the sanctity of the doctor-patient privilege, as recognized by the State of California and its licensing authorities.

Dr. Weiss: Mr. Simpson, do you understand what I've just said?

Mr. Simpson: Uh-huh. Yes.

Dr. Weiss: Just for the record, can I get you to say that you agree to being recorded? For the record.

Mr. Simpson: It's okay for Dr. Weiss to record this session.

Dr. Weiss: Thank you. Mr. Simpson, we've never met before, but of course I know something about you. Tell me how you happen to be here today.

Mr. Simpson: Well, I was referred. I was referred by my medical doctor.

Dr. Weiss: I see. Was there a reason that he referred you to me?

Mr. Simpson: Well, yeah. It was health-related. And he thought you could maybe help me.

Dr. Weiss: When you say "health-related," what do you mean, exactly?

Mr. Simpson: It's . . . I've been having a problem, kind of a problem, anyway. . . .

Dr. Weiss: I need to ask you to be a little more specific.

Mr. Simpson: It involves . . . it's a sexual thing, you know?

Dr. Weiss: Mr. Simpson . . . may I call you O.J.?

Mr. Simpson: Sure.

A Work of Fiction

Dr. Weiss: O.J., I'm sure you know this is an area that I've done quite a bit of work and study in, human sexuality in general and, specifically, male sexual function. That's probably why you were referred to me.

Mr. Simpson: I think so. Right.

Dr. Weiss: So the sexual problem you're experiencing, does it involve your ability to be satisfied?

Mr. Simpson: Uh-huh.

Dr. Weiss: Can you have an orgasm?

Mr. Simpson: Yeah. But it takes ... work. More than I'm used to.

Dr. Weiss: So, then, you've had some difficulty getting an erection?

Mr. Simpson: I can get one. It just isn't as ... well, you know. Hard.

Dr. Weiss: All right. I need to get a little background information from you, first. Tell me about your family, O.J. Let's start with your father.

Mr. Simpson: He's dead.

Dr. Weiss: Is that all? He's dead. When did he die?

Mr. Simpson: Don't know: '85, '86. Something like that.

Dr. Weiss: Were you and he close?

Mr. Simpson: Sure.

Dr. Weiss: Tell me about him.

Mr. Simpson: Well, what do you want to know? I mean he was a good guy. Great cook. My son takes after him. My son Jason is a chef.

The Confession of O.J. Simpson

Dr. Weiss: What was the relationship between him and your mother?

Mr. Simpson: Oh. They were okay, I guess. They stayed friends.

Dr. Weiss: Stayed friends?

Mr. Simpson: Yeah, I mean after he left.

Dr. Weiss: I'm sorry. I didn't understand they were divorced.

Mr. Simpson: Well, they never were, really. He just left when I was four.

Dr. Weiss: I see.

Mr. Simpson: He still came around a lot. We saw him at Thanksgiving and Christmas and in church. And sometimes my momma called him to come over and give me a whippin' when I needed it.

Dr. Weiss: Why did he and your mother separate, do you know?

Mr. Simpson: Oh, I don't know. Different things, I guess. He wanted his own kind of life.

Dr. Weiss: What do you mean?

Mr. Simpson: Hey, man. I don't know what he wanted. What has this got to do with me anyway? I didn't come here to talk about him.

Dr. Weiss: Let me take a minute and try and explain how this could help. You're familiar, I take it, with the need to establish a patient's medical history. That's why your doctor asks you if anyone in your family has a history of, say, heart disease. Or diabetes.

A Work of Fiction

Mr. Simpson: Uh-huh.

Dr. Weiss: Well, what I'm trying to do here is much the same thing.

Mr. Simpson: You mean like my thing could be inherited?

Dr. Weiss: Possibly. Sexual function is often related to physical health. How is your health, by the way?

Mr. Simpson: Great. I play golf every day. I feel great. Oh, you know, there's the arthritis. That does run in my family. But it ain't too bad. I got this product, JuicePlus, you know, that helps me.

Dr. Weiss: Are you taking any medications? Any prescriptions?

Mr. Simpson: Not right now. Sometimes Xanax to help me sleep.

Dr. Weiss: Alcohol?

Mr. Simpson: I drink sometimes. Not a lot. When we go out.

Dr. Weiss: How about drugs?

Mr. Simpson: That's not a problem for me.

Dr. Weiss: You don't use them, then.

Mr. Simpson: Not really.

Dr. Weiss: I know this may seem personal, but remember everything you say to me will remain completely confidential. By "not really," I take it you mean that you have used drugs in the past?

Mr. Simpson: Yeah.

The Confession of O. J. Simpson

Dr. Weiss: Any recent use?

Mr. Simpson: I've done cocaine a couple times in the last few months. Nothing major.

Dr. Weiss: All right. Let's go back to your father for just a minute more. You said you were close to him?

Mr. Simpson: Yeah, we got along all right. I wouldn't say we were real close or anything. Not like my mom, anyway. But he came down here to visit sometimes. He and Nicole really got along.

Dr. Weiss: That's your wife?

Mr. Simpson: Yes. Well, she's technically my ex-wife, but we're sort of back together.

Dr. Weiss: Tell me something you liked about your father.

Mr. Simpson: Something I liked?

Dr. Weiss: Yes.

Mr. Simpson: I don't know. Like I said, he could cook real good. He was funny. Good with my kids. They loved him. I don't know.

Dr. Weiss: Is there anything in particular that you didn't like about him?

Mr. Simpson: No.

Dr. Weiss: Nothing?

A Work of Fiction

Mr. Simpson:	Look, what do you want to know? I mean, this ain't . . . Okay, you want to know what I didn't like about him? He embarrassed my family, that's what I didn't like. He fucking humiliated my mother, that's what I didn't like. And when he left, he didn't go far enough away, that's what I didn't like.
Dr. Weiss:	I don't understand.
Mr. Simpson:	Are you deaf? He was a fairy, okay? Are you happy? Is that what you wanted me to say?
Dr. Weiss:	O.J., I know this is hard. But stay with me here for a minute. This could be important in figuring out how to help you.
Mr. Simpson:	I don't care.
Dr. Weiss:	Did your mother know your father was gay?
Mr. Simpson:	Yeah.
Dr. Weiss:	You have brothers and sisters, right?
Mr. Simpson:	Two sisters and a brother.
Dr. Weiss:	Did they know?
Mr. Simpson:	Yeah.
Dr. Weiss:	So this is why—
Mr. Simpson:	Everybody knew, man. The whole god-damned neighborhood knew. The kids at school. "Hey, O.J.! How's yo momma? The one with the dick!"
Dr. Weiss:	Kids can be cruel. So, it's been hard for you to forgive him?
Mr. Simpson:	Oh, I forgive him. I don't know if God did, though.

31

The Confession of O. J. Simpson

Dr. Weiss: What do you mean?

Mr. Simpson: He got AIDS, man. He got AIDS from being fucked up the ass too many times. God sent him a message.

Dr. Weiss: You believe that?

Mr. Simpson: It's not what I believe. It's what the Bible says.

Dr. Weiss: Before he died, how long had it been since you'd last seen him?

Mr. Simpson: Oh man, that really was the hand of God. He was sick in the hospital in San Francisco and I just decided to go see him. I mean, I didn't think he was that sick or nothin'. I knew he was gonna die, but I didn't know right away. So I just flew up there and walked in. Didn't call. My sisters were there. And he died five minutes after I got there. Like he was waiting for me.

Dr. Weiss: Did he know you were there?

Mr. Simpson: Yeah. That was the great thing, man. He knew. He knew. I held his hand. God gave me that time with him.

Dr. Weiss: I'd like to try and focus on specifically what brought you here today. How long have you noticed difficulty in sustaining an erection?

Mr. Simpson: It's been a couple . . . two or three times now.

Dr. Weiss: And this has been with your ex-wife . . . Nicole?

A Work of Fiction

Mr. Simpson: Yeah. And once with my girlfriend, too. Paula. This never happened to me before, doc. I never had any problems. You can ask a lot of girls, they'll all tell you that's the truth. You think I'm sick or something?

Dr. Weiss: That's what we're going to try and find out. You say this has happened with both Nicole and . . . Paula, is it?

Mr. Simpson: Yes.

Dr. Weiss: Is there any unusual tension you're experiencing? The reconciliation with your wife, has it been stressful?

Mr. Simpson: Sometimes. A little. Then other times it's great.

Dr. Weiss: Does Nicole know of your involvement with Paula?

Mr. Simpson: Yeah. She don't like her much.

Dr. Weiss: They've met?

Mr. Simpson: A couple of times. Mostly by accident. When I was just with Paula, we ran into Nicole. I told Nicole that she should give Paula a chance, that she's a nice girl, but she didn't want to hear it.

Dr. Weiss: So it's over now with you and Paula?

Mr. Simpson: I think so. I'm not sure Paula thinks that. You know, it's too bad, Nicole don't like Paula. That would solve a lot of problems.

Dr. Weiss: How do you mean?

33

Mr. Simpson:	I could have 'em both. Wouldn't that be great? I mean they're both beautiful girls, man. Nicole's got blond hair and Paula is dark. Her hair, I mean. They would be so hot together. Probably solve all my problems. Then I wouldn't need to see you, would I?
Dr. Weiss:	Well, it would be nice if it were that easy. We're at the end of the hour. I'd like to see you again next week.
Mr. Simpson:	I'm not sure if I'm in town. I'll have my secretary call you.
Dr. Weiss:	That would be fine. There's one thing, O.J., before you go, if you could. My son's a big fan of yours. Could you sign this for him?
Mr. Simpson:	Sure. What's his name?
Dr. Weiss:	Michael.
Mr. Simpson:	Here you go.
Dr. Weiss:	Thanks. I appreciate it. I'll look forward to hearing from your secretary, then.
Mr. Simpson:	Sure.
	End of transcription.

Jesus. I heard myself exhaling when I finished. He'd been watching me carefully while I'd read it. Now he was waiting for me to say something.

"Why did he record it?" I asked a neutral question, hoping to stay away from any discussion of what I'd just read.

"He said he thought it would help me understand what was

wrong with me. What an *asshole*. I made sure I got the original tape back from him, too.''

"Did you ever see him again?''

"Are you kidding? He was just another jock sniffer. Could you tell how hot he was getting when I was talking about Nicole and Paula together? Anyway, the reason I went to see him—that don't matter anymore. It was just that one time. It was probably some kind of virus or some shit like that. I mean sometimes it would be a big *help* if my dick didn't work so good, you see what I'm sayin'?''

I did. But I didn't want to think about the implications. I looked at my watch. Ten minutes after one. He'd been here not quite two hours, yet everything I'd understood about my life when I woke up that morning had just shifted out from under me. I didn't need this now. My practice was very shaky. The court case next week was a must-win for me. I knew I should back out now, tell him I didn't want any part of this. But I also knew I wouldn't. How had it come to this?

I needed the money.

CHAPTER FOUR

Rachel used to say, "If there's money involved, Sam Roosevelt will find a way *not* to make it." When we were still in college—Berkeley—she had said it with humor, even admiration. By the time we were divorced, she said it with a tired edge in her voice. I couldn't blame her, really. She'd put up with a lot just by staying married to me.

Rachel supported both of us when I was in law school, and hadn't complained—very much—when, after passing the bar, I decided to go *back* to school and get my Ph.D. When Laura was born, we'd already been together ten years, eight of them married, and I had been a student the entire time. "The Eleven-Year Man," was what she called me when she wanted to *utz* me (a Yiddish word that, although difficult to translate, means something like "get my goat"). And, toward the end, she utzed me with unerring skill. She'd say, "You're a Jew *and* you're poor. How is that possible?"

It had always been a particular source of frustration to her that we had such a prominent American name and nothing tangible to show for it. Another familiar refrain of Rachel's was "You *would* have the same name as the guy on the *dime*."

I had long ago made a separate peace with my famous, if irrelevant, surname. It was helpful in restaurants—especially in New York and Washington—and annoying at cocktail parties. (My favorite "Roosevelt moment" was when, after having patiently explained for the umpteenth time that my family tree had neither a Franklin nor a Theodore in any branch, Rachel's aunt said to me: "Then you *must* be related to Eleanor.")

But Melvin Belli had loved my name. The ancient-but-still-legendary lawyer and self-proclaimed "King of Torts" couldn't care less that I wasn't a presidential descendant. ("Nobody will know if we don't tell them, Sam," he said conspiratorially to me during our first meeting—he had actually *winked*.) He'd hired me on the spot, without even glancing at my résumé.

After less than a year of working for him (no one worked *with* Melvin Belli), I had what Rachel derisively referred to as an "attack of ethics." I went to Belli and told him, rather self-righteously, that I still thought law was something to be practiced in court, not in a hospital waiting room. He remained silent throughout my short speech, stroking the coat of one of those obnoxious black whippets that seemed never to leave his side (unless it was to drop a "present" on my office rug—one of the other perks of the Belli firm).

When I was done he said, "Sam, I applaud your integrity. I can afford to admire it in you for the very reason that I can't tolerate it anywhere else around here. If I did, it would break me. But you wear it well, my boy. It fits you, like a good suit of clothes. And that's good for business. That's why I'm making you a partner." I was stunned. I had gone into his office fully expecting to quit and I walked out with my name on the door.

The partnership lasted until the day I discovered, to my horror, what he'd meant when he said he couldn't afford integrity anywhere else. It turned out that for the last several years he'd been systematically looting the partnership's coffers for his personal use. When I tried to confront him on this, he refused to see me.

I suddenly found myself out of a job (I moved what was left of my practice into our house) and facing the daunting task of suing Belli for my share of the partnership, which amounted to more than $750,000. I certainly couldn't afford a lawyer (or even a paralegal) to handle the suit, so I was forced to do it all myself. Then, after two years of arduous preparation, my efforts were rendered meaningless. Melvin Belli, for whom image had always been everything, surprised everyone by filing for bankruptcy. I was now forced into a very long line of creditors that included two of Belli's five ex-wives. All of us understood that it would be nearly impossible to recover any funds from the now-dethroned King of Torts.

Just when it seemed that things couldn't possibly get worse, Rachel filed for divorce. Our marriage had been running on fumes for some time, but Belli's bankruptcy was more than she could take. She had been surviving on the faint hope of a three-quarter-million-dollar windfall that would relieve our tremendous financial pressures and turn our lives around. Despite my warnings that our chances of ever seeing that money were remote at best, she'd come to fixate on the Belli suit as the solution to all our problems. When Belli went "Belli-up" (as the newspapers gleefully described it; worse, Rachel got the news with her morning coffee, before I could break it to her), she withdrew completely. There were no more fights, no arguing. Just silence. Then, a few days later, Rachel quietly told me she'd filed for divorce. It wasn't a subject open for discussion; just a fact, like what the weather would be that day or who would be coming for dinner on Saturday night. A *fait accompli*.

In a way, the divorce wasn't that hard for either of us to accept. Although we had never talked about it in so many words, we both knew only two things had remained consistently strong in our marriage: our friendship (which, since we both wanted to preserve it, essentially *required* we get a divorce) and the tremendous love we both had—have—for our daughter.

When we couldn't seem to agree on anything else, we usually chose to talk about Laura. She was our bridge, our glue. And, from a very early age, this fact had not been lost on Laura. Being an only child, she'd received virtually all our attention since the day we brought her home from the hospital. Even as a little girl, she had a keen sense of her importance to Rachel and me. She knew our devotion to her was an unending source of joy in our lives. And with her quick, intuitive mind, she played on that knowledge whenever she sensed there was any trouble brewing between her mother and me.

I remember once, when she was about four or five, I was pushing Laura in the swing set we'd bought for the backyard. "Higher, Daddy. Push me higher!" Without warning, on the swing's upward arc, she went flying out and landed, about fifteen feet away, on the lawn. Panicked, I raced over to her. Fortunately, she'd landed on all fours and the grass had cushioned her fall. She wasn't crying. She seemed more stunned than hurt. I picked her up in my arms and held her tight to my chest. "Oh, my God, baby. Are you all right?" I was shouting and tears were running down my face. Laura managed a little smile to let me know she was okay.

Then Rachel—who'd been inside the house when this happened—came running out. She'd heard me shouting.

"What is it! What's wrong? Oh my God, Sam! What happened? What did you *do*?"

"She . . . fell . . . fell out of the swing." I was having trouble catching my breath.

"How could you let that happen? Weren't you *watching* her?"

Suddenly I wasn't upset anymore about Laura. I was getting angry at Rachel for her accusatory tone.

"Of course I was watching her. I always watch her when you're too goddamned busy to spend any time with her. Where the hell were *you*?"

Laura, who had been taking all this in, looked first at me,

then at her mother. Then, for the first time, *she* began crying. Hard and uncontrollably.

Rachel and I looked at each other and we both knew immediately what had happened. Laura was fine, thank God. But she could tell we weren't. And if it took her tears to get us to stop fighting, she was more than happy to oblige.

It naturally followed when Rachel and I were preparing to divorce, it would be Laura who'd try to get us to change our minds. She used charm ("I'm too beautiful to have divorced parents"), guilt ("I hate you both. You're both so *selfish*"), threats ("I won't go to college, then how will you feel?"), and imprecations ("Please, Dad. I love you so much and I want you to live with us"). When none of it worked, something seemed to change about our beloved daughter. She developed a certain wistfulness about her, as if she'd passed through some invisible boundary between childhood and adulthood.

Faced with the twin prospects of alimony and child support (and the responsibility of paying for Laura's impending college education; she'd been accepted to Harvard for the fall term), I had no choice but to pursue Melvin Belli in bankruptcy court. I needed that partnership money desperately.

But as it happened, Belli had one last royal card up his sleeve: the king of spades. Six months after declaring bankruptcy, Melvin Belli filed his own permanent change of venue at the age of eighty-eight. This left his estate as the defendant, and although Belli himself was no longer an obstacle, his death meant that it would be even harder to find out just where he'd squirreled away the money he had stolen from me and his other partners. Now, after more than four years, my case was finally going to be heard, and I'd been putting all my time and energy into preparing for it. If I didn't win, it was more than likely that I'd soon be appearing in that same bankruptcy court again, only this time it would not be as a plaintiff.

The phone rang on my desk, startling both Simpson and me. I looked at it and saw it was my private line, the same number that he'd called me on that morning. I let it ring.

"Aren't you gonna answer it?"

"No, I'll let the machine pick up."

After the fourth ring, the answering machine clicked on and I heard my voice say, *"I'm sorry I'm not here to take your call right now. Please leave a message and I'll call you back as soon as I can. Thanks for calling."* Then, after the brief, high-pitched tone, came another voice: "Sam. *Sam.* SAM! Goddammit, Sam Roosevelt, pick up this phone. I know you're there."

It was Rachel. I looked at Simpson, who was smiling at me as if I had suddenly become one of his "boys." I didn't pick up the phone.

"All right, Sam. You know we had a deal. I can't live like this. If I don't get my check and Laura's check by tomorrow, I'll see you in court. You remember court, don't you, Sam? It's that place where you're supposed to be working for a living." Her voice was steeped in sarcasm. She was using that tone which had come to sound like fingernails on a blackboard to me.

Then she broke. *"I'm not kidding, Sam. I mean it this time."*

She was crying now, and I knew this was making her even angrier. *"Are you listening to me, Sam! I mean it, goddamn you!"*

The sound of her slamming down the receiver made me wince. Simpson, who seemed to sense he'd just regained the upper hand with me, shrugged and, without a trace of irony, said what men always say in these situations: "Women. What are you gonna do? Can't live with 'em, can't live without 'em."

I didn't respond. Instead I looked down at the black binder that was still open on my desk and made a mental calculation of what twenty-five percent of fifteen million was.

CHAPTER FIVE

I said to him, "If you really want me to go through all of this, it's going to take a while. Why don't you go back to the condo and I'll call you when I'm finished. Is there still a phone—"

Before I could finish my question, he was on his feet, standing over my desk.

"No way, Sam. I'm not going anywhere. Like I told you, *nobody* has seen this stuff before. Now it's just you. Don't get me wrong, it's not that I don't trust you. I'm not sayin' that at all. I *do* trust you. But like you seen, there's lots of personal stuff and shit that could be . . . it could be *misunderstood*. So if I stay here when you're reading it, I can keep explaining all about what it means. You see what I'm sayin'?"

I did. He *didn't* trust me. But there was no point in my calling him on it. He'd just deny it and I had already crossed my Rubicon. I had chosen, at least for now, to be one of his

45

"boys." It would serve no useful purpose to confront him—
certainly not over the issue of whether *he* trusted *me*.

Instead, I looked up at him sharply and said, "So, you're
planning on just standing there all day and reading over my
shoulder?" My tone made it plain that I didn't intend for this to
happen.

"No, man. You go ahead. I'll just hang out. You got anything in the house to eat?"

My mother would have been ashamed. "I'm sorry. I should
have offered you something before. Let's go downstairs. I'll fix
you a sandwich."

I closed the binder and put it in my top desk drawer. He
watched me do this, but said nothing.

We went downstairs to the kitchen and I soon found myself
standing over a cutting board, chopping an onion and fixing a
tuna-salad sandwich for Orenthal James Simpson.

He was leaning against my refrigerator, drinking casually
from a can of Coke, as if we were old friends and he'd been
doing this for years.

"You got a nice house, Sam. This is a good neighborhood,
Noe Valley. Good for kids."

Despite all that had happened to him, O. J. Simpson still
possessed an almost preternatural ability to seem at ease in any
situation. This extraordinary talent served a dual purpose for
Simpson: it allowed him to keep functioning in virtually any
circumstance, no matter how hostile; and he also used it to dis-
arm even those who were predisposed not to feel comfortable
around him—like me.

"You own this place?"

A touchy subject. Rachel had agreed to let me stay in the house because it was also my office, but only for a year. That year was up next month, and I either had to buy out her half interest or we had to sell the house and divide the money.

"Sort of. My wife . . . my ex-wife and I own it—I may be putting it on the market soon." I wiped an onion tear with my sleeve.

"Life's a bitch, ain't it?" He said this gently, even sympathetically. There was no malice or anger in his voice. He was attempting to feel my pain. This triggered a thought and I used it to change the subject.

"What was all that stuff before about Clinton?"

I handed Simpson his sandwich and started fixing one for myself. A mouth full of food didn't stop him from answering my question.

"You wanna know why I'm pissed?" This came out as "piffed." "Okay, here's what happened. About three weeks before Nicole . . . died . . . I was in D.C., and the president—Big Bill *himself,* not some assistant—calls me and asks do I want to play a round of golf with him on Sunday? I said sure, even though I was supposed to leave on Saturday and I had to change my flights all around. But I said sure, I'd do it. I mean, he's the *president,* right?"

He paused and said, "That sandwich was great. You got anything else?"

Having grabbed another Coke, he was now scrounging through my refrigerator looking for more food. I knew the pickings were slim—I mostly got takeout these days—so I said, "Here, take this," and handed him the sandwich I'd just made for myself.

"So I get to the golf course at six forty-five on Sunday morning and there's all these Secret Service guys there." He'd immediately resumed telling his story without the slightest acknowledgment that he had just eaten my lunch. He was a piece of work.

"I'm on the list and I get cleared in and we're supposed to be teeing off at seven. Do you know what time he got there? Eight-thirty! He was an *hour and a half late.* I couldn't believe it. The Secret Service guys were like all apologetic and kept sayin', 'Sorry, Juice. He does this all the time.' And I told them it wasn't their fault and this one guy—I knew him from when I met Bush—he said, 'You should see what happens when he keeps his wife waiting. Boy, does she let him have it.' And I said, 'I'll bet she's a real "*Bill*buster" ' and they all thought that was the funniest damn thing they ever heard."

I finished fixing another sandwich. This one I definitely intended to eat. I motioned him in the direction of my small dining-room table and we went in and sat down. He kept right on talking.

"Anyway, Clinton finally shows up and he apologizes for bein' late, said how he had to go to an early church service, but he hoped I didn't mind waiting. Now, what am I gonna *say*? 'Fuck you, you rude cracker?' "

I listened to all this without comment, but I did think how happy Rush Limbaugh would be right now.

A Work of Fiction

Simpson was drumming the fingers of his right hand on the tabletop as he spoke, the rhythm growing more rapid as he grew more agitated.

"So we finished the first nine holes—I was up by three strokes by the way, he ain't very good—and he turns to me and says, 'I really hope we get to do this again soon.' He's *leavin'*. I couldn't believe it. He keeps me waiting almost two hours, then he only plays nine holes? I mean, what an *asshole*."

"What did you say to him?" My question was purely rhetorical. There was virtually no chance he wouldn't tell me.

"I was very respectful to him, like my momma always taught me. I said, 'Mr. President, it's been an honor. Anytime you want, I'm there. Can I get you to do me one favor, though? My wife, she'd love a picture of you and me together.' And, he says, 'Sure. No problem. What's her name? I'll sign it for her.' So we take the picture, he's got his arm around me and he has this weird grin that looks like he's biting his lip, and I tell him to make it out to Nicole. This kid who goes everywhere with him, he writes that down, and Clinton, that lying *motherfucker,* he says 'We'll send that to you right away.' "

He was on his feet again and I didn't want a repeat of the scene in my office.

"Take it easy, O.J.," I said. "So you never got the picture, is that what this is all about?"

"NO!" He slammed his open palm down hard on the tabletop, rattling the plates. "It's not about *me,* man. *Nicole* never got to see it. She would have been real impressed and she never got to see it. It never came. To this day, I never got it."

49

The Confession of O.J. Simpson

And we both knew he never would. My guess was that by now the White House had burned the negatives and transferred the photographer to a permanent detail on Guam.

"But I got him back, that bastard . . . what goes around, comes around." He wasn't raging anymore. In fact, he began to gloat.

"You remember. He was giving his big speech on the state of the country . . . state of the *union* that's what it's called— anyway, that was the exact time my civil jury came back with a verdict. I beat him *bad,* man. Fox cut away from him to cover *me.* NBC went split screen. Where we went head to head, I got a twenty-two rating and a thirty-four share. I cleaned his *clock.*"

This was too much to take.

"But, O.J., look what kind of coverage you were *getting.* It's not exactly like you won the Super Bowl that day."

He surprised me by not reacting defensively to what I'd said. Instead, he smiled and shrugged his shoulders. When he spoke, his tone was even and he sounded expansive.

"Oh, sure, man. I *know* I didn't win with that jury. No way I was ever gonna win with *that* jury, no matter what I did. Everybody knew that. But that don't matter. I'll get it back. Like the Bible says, I'll get it back seven times more. Just like Clinton got *his* back. Don't let anybody ever tell you there ain't no justice in life, Sam. Ask Clinton. Ask Big Bill."

We were still sitting at my dining-room table, and rather than engage him further in a discussion of either Bill Clinton or justice, I rose and took our plates, my glass, and his empty Coke can into the kitchen.

A Work of Fiction

I put the dishes in the sink (they were really starting to pile up; when was my housekeeper coming?), then started back into the dining room, but he had followed me into the kitchen.

"Hey, Sam. You're a fuckin' slob, man." He was smiling. "You can't be giving us bachelors a bad name."

Then, bizarre as it may sound, O. J. Simpson moved around me, stepped up to the sink, and began washing a week's worth of my dirty dishes.

Stunned and a little embarrassed by his gesture, I said, "Hey, you don't have to do that. I've got somebody coming in to take care of—"

He cut me off. "Shut up, Sam. This'll take five minutes. Grab a towel and you can dry."

Since he was already up to his well-muscled forearms in soap and water, I knew it was pointless to argue with him. I took a dish towel from the rack and he started passing me plates.

And, of course, he kept talking.

"You know what you was just saying before, about what kind of TV coverage I've been getting?"

I nodded as he handed me a fistful of silverware. He was *racing* through those dishes.

"You know what Johnnie Cochran says—I call him Johnnie *King* now 'cause he's like some kind of *messiah* to black folk— he's marching down in Selma—he's *loving* all this attention he gets from being my lawyer—remember *I* hired him—anyway, Johnnie thinks my situation is just like Nixon's was after the media crucified him. And he came back. He came all the way

51

back. When he died, he was a *statesman*, man. A national fucking *treasure*.''

He continued, ''You know a lot of people wanted *me* to run for office. Republicans did. They thought I'd be a great candidate, too. I was gonna do it. I could've run for the state senate. 'Senator Simpson.' That sounds good, don't it?''

I listened to all this with detachment and not a little amusement. Were he not so completely self-involved, Simpson would have noticed the slight smile I couldn't contain when he'd compared himself with Nixon. And it probably would have offended him. Having toiled in my share of campaigns, I knew something about politics and politicians. When Rachel and I were at Berkeley we'd both worked for McGovern. Although I was still only an undergraduate, I'd actually been hired to prepare some of McGovern's briefing materials in the unlikely event that Nixon would agree to debate him. Although there was never a debate, I learned a lot—more than I cared to—about Richard Nixon.

Which is why I knew that Simpson's comparison of himself with Nixon, while absurdly self-aggrandizing on its face, was, in another way, weirdly accurate. I was also sure that Simpson wouldn't care to examine their similarities too closely: both were self-made men who had fought their way up from hardscrabble beginnings to reach the absolute pinnacle of their chosen professions; both had strong mothers with deep religious convictions from whom they had trouble separating in adulthood; both drank too much and both talked too much (especially when there was a tape recorder running); both were responsible for their own precipitous fall from public grace and both were obsessed with finding a way back from the depths.

But that's also where—despite Johnnie Cochran's optimism—the comparison stopped. Nixon, for all his flaws, had an intellect that allowed him to be of value even after his public disgrace. Once he had retired from football, Simpson could *only* trade on the one quality he would now never again possess: his likability. And, unlike Nixon, who understood how reviled he was and how that necessitated his careful reemergence into the public eye over a period of many years, Simpson seemed incapable of fully appreciating how despised he was. Sure, he talked about how he was ''hated'' or how people ''lied'' to him, but in the same breath he was weaving fantastic scenarios about how his rating ''numbers'' were so great that he could still command—and deliver—a television audience whenever he chose.

Almost as if he'd been listening to my thoughts, Simpson leaned toward me over the sink. His body language seemed to say that he was about to take me into his confidence in a way he hadn't yet done.

''You know, Sam, I still *could*.'' He was excited, but not out of control. He spoke quickly, almost breathlessly. ''I got no conviction. I can still vote. So I *could* run. Wouldn't that be a *mind fuck* for the press, man? Johnnie says I could get elected anywhere in the country where there's a black-majority district. Marion Barry did it. That congressman in Florida, he did it, even after they already *impeached* his ass when he was a judge.''

I didn't know how to respond to him. Nothing I could think

of seemed remotely adequate to the moment. Pointing out to him that neither Barry nor the congressman from Florida had been accused of—let alone found liable for—the crime of *murder,* would be meaningless. Right now he was so disconnected from anything approaching reality he probably wouldn't even comprehend the words I might use to challenge his delusions of restored honor.

Instead, I changed the subject. I said, "Listen, if I'm ever going to read all that material and make sense of it . . . I'd better get started on it now."

If he was disappointed I wasn't offering to manage his campaign, he didn't let on. He gave me a little half-smile and said, "You're the boss. Let's do it."

He walked ahead of me through the dining room and out into my living room. Along the far wall was a row of bookcases. To the left of these was a glass cabinet that contained my stereo system and CDs. The furnishings were sparse. Rachel had let me stay in the house, but she'd taken most of "her" furniture to the apartment she and Laura were renting in a restored Victorian in the Haight. The only things she'd left behind in this room—a green Naugahyde couch and an overstuffed chair—were the two pieces she'd always hated.

Simpson went directly to the stereo cabinet and began looking through my CD collection. I lingered in the dining-room doorway and looked at my watch. It was already after two o'clock.

"O.J., I'm heading upstairs. Will you be all right down here?"

A Work of Fiction

"*Jesus,* Sam! Is all your taste in your mouth?" He turned around and waved a CD case in the air. Michael Bolton. "What is *this* shit, man?"

"My wife likes him. She must've left it." I wasn't about to tell him it was mine.

"What do chicks *see* in him? He's a fuckin' *freak*. And that hair! *Putz.*" He spat this last word out, sounding just like my uncle Harry in Miami Beach.

"Now, *this*. This is *music*." He was holding *Sinatra's Greatest Hits*. He popped it into the CD player.

Simpson crossed to the bookshelves, singing along. " 'My kind of town, Chicago is. My kind of town . . .' " He had a terrible voice. He reached up and pulled a black-and-white volume off the top shelf. It was *The Godfather*.

"I love this book. This is the *greatest* book."

He sat down with the book and started turning the pages. Before I could move toward the stairs, he suddenly jumped up, the book falling on the couch, and ran past me into the kitchen. I heard the refrigerator door open and close. When he came back into the room, he had an orange in his hand. He reached into his pants pocket and pulled out what appeared to be a Swiss army knife. In a single swift motion he opened and locked the blade. Then he cut a triangular wedge slice from the orange.

"Remember this scene from the movie, Sam?"

Brando-like, he put the orange slice, peel out, in his mouth. His face was now contorted in a macabre orange smile and he moved toward me menacingly, with his arms outstretched—like a jack-o'-lantern with limbs. Suddenly he grabbed his chest, and feigning the famous Corleone heart attack, he collapsed in laughter on my couch.

I shook my head at all this and said, "I'm glad you're amusing yourself." Then I crossed the room and started upstairs.

As I reached the landing he called out, "Hey, Sam! I always wanted to know what it'd be like to make someone an offer they couldn't refuse!" He was still laughing when I closed the office door behind me.

CHAPTER SIX

It was getting dark outside, although it was still only the middle of the afternoon. I crossed to the window, stopping to (carefully) pick up the Clinton photo and frame, which remained on the floor where he'd flung them.

The early gloom was arriving in the form of storm clouds that appeared ready to burst at any moment. I closed the window, and after unraveling the cord, which he'd twisted into a dozen little knots, I drew the venetian blinds as well. My office was now completely dark, save for a sliver of light that leaked in from under the closed door.

I switched on the green-shaded desk lamp that Rachel always said was an affectation designed to make me *feel* like a legal scholar. Then I sat down and removed the book from the top middle drawer of my desk, placing it in the center of the desktop blotter. I took out my reading glasses and once again opened his "pot of gold." This time I removed the loose pages and letters and set them all to one side. What remained were the original sheets that had come with the binder. They were white three-hole pages, lined, and there appeared to be about fifty of them in the book.

What seemed to make sense was for me to start by organizing the loose pages into something approaching an order. I set Dr. Weiss's transcript aside, then began sorting the yellow legal pages. As I turned them around and right side up, I noticed most of them were either from 1994 or 1995. The criminal trial. Hadn't there been some discussion about what had happened to all those notes Simpson was seen taking in court? Although I'd obviously seen some of the criminal trial on TV—who could avoid it?—for the first time I was now beginning to wish I'd paid closer attention to it. I thought I remembered they'd been subpoenaed for the civil trial and it turned out they were "lost." Maybe they weren't so lost anymore.

Here was one, dated *"1/18/95"*:

I can not believe that my life is on the line and these ass-holes are fighting like 2 little kids This is the Nightmare Team! If Gil and Marcia know how bad this is they would have got the death penalty. This is crazy! Shapiro wont even look at Lee. They dont speak even to say hello. I told Shapiro that Im not paying him 100 grand every month to fight with my lawyers. He's supposed to be fighting Marcia and Darden. Their the enemy! Shapiro kept saying over and over and over so Im sick of hearing about it that Lee is a snake and we have to get rid of him. He is godfather to my son and he betrayed me. Give me a fucking break! I'm the guy sitting in jail and For What? Shapiro thinks Lee talked to the press maybe he did? I agree with him that we cant have leaks and I gave Lee hell about it. He says it wasnt him so who knows who is a liar? It dont matter if they hate each other I told them that I played football with lots of guys I didnt like and you put that shit aside when its game time. This is game time for ME!!!

Another yellow page had MARCIA CLARK in bold letters across the top. Beneath that he'd written:

2/12/95 Shes not fooling anybody. The way she comes on to Johnnie. The little giggles and cutesy shit. She is playing for the camera like this is an audition to her. I bet when this is all over she wants to be an actress. The jury dont like any of her acting they can see thru her. Id like a chance to go one on one with her. See who comes out on top. I know that the lawyers are probably right that if I say something on the stand once I could forget to say it the exact same way on cross exam. But she has this attitude that makes me want to knock that chip off her shoulder.

He didn't care much for Lance Ito either. I had to smile a little at Simpson's characterization of him. Ito and I had been classmates in law school at Berkeley. I hadn't known him well, but we were in one study group together. Even then he was a bit starstruck. I have a distinct memory of him missing an important study session to attend a lecture on campus. The guest speaker was . . . *Burt Reynolds*. The next day in class he showed everybody Reynolds's autograph. Simpson seemed to have a similar perception of Ito:

> *Judge Ego was doing his thing again today. He rules against us all the time like he made up his mind even before Johnnie is done. And he is in such a hurry sometimes to get off his big chair and go to chambers. Maybe Larry King is coming! Or Richard Dryfus! Or Connie Fucking Chung who I hate for what she did to Momma. Judge Ego is a lot like Marcia. They can have a TV show together like Regis and Cathy Lee.*

How had he managed to keep these to himself? I wondered. Hadn't anyone *seen* what he was writing? This next one was apparently a Knute Rockne speech to his "players." It was undated, but the heading was in memo form:

TO:　　　　TEAM
FROM:　　　OJ
SUBJECT:　STRATEGY

In it, he continued a recurring theme with his attorneys, which seemed to be "I'm smarter than you guys. *And* I'm paying you. You *better* listen to me." Or, with regard to the prosecution, it was "I've hired lawyers who can kick your ass. Why don't you just figure that out and give up now?" For example:

I know we're in the last quarter. This is where we separate the men from the boys. You too Marcia. Guys, we are ahead. We cant make mistakes. Darden fumbled the glove. The jury hates Marcia. Did you see those women looking at her? They dont like her hair. They dont trust nothing she says. I know this. Just keep it together now. You guys are the best. I know because Im paying for you. And your worth it. We are going to win. I know that for one reason: I did not do this. You know that. Now I want you to make the jury know that.

The clouds broke and I heard the downpour begin outside. Usually when it rained, I would linger—sometimes for hours— just listening to the steady, reassuring sound. Right now it didn't provide any comfort.

I returned to the business at hand. I'd now read or skimmed most of the yellow pages and clearly they were all written during the criminal trial. Despite his candid observations about the courtroom players, there was virtually no commentary on the case itself, unless you counted his constant refrain of "Why am I here? I didn't *do* this." I reasoned that perhaps the journal had originally been purchased by him as a way to record his thoughts about June 12. Maybe another psychiatrist, assuming his inno-cence, of course, thought such a process might "help him."

I picked up the journal and pulled it closer, holding it up at an angle in front of me, the way you'd read a book. This action shook something free from the back of the binder; an envelope fell on my desk. I thought I'd removed all the loose materials, but I must have missed this.

The envelope was small and square and of a size that might normally contain a greeting card. It was addressed to *Mr. O. J. Simpson, 360 N. Rockingham, Los Angeles, California 90049.* Each letter *O* and all of the zeroes had been filled in with two dots above a half circle, the symbol of a smiling face.

There was no return address on the front, but it had been postmarked in Los Angeles. I pulled out two sheets of lavender-colored paper. They'd been folded three times so that they could fit into the envelope. Inside the two sheets was another one of those little microcassette tapes, like the ones I'd seen (and which still remained) in the back pocket of the binder.

I turned the envelope over, still looking for a return address. Although there wasn't one, I couldn't fail to recognize the by-now-familiar penmanship of O. J. Simpson. In his hand, in block letters, he'd printed the words: *LIAR! LISTEN TO THE TAPE!*

The letter itself, which covered both sides of each sheet of lavender stationery, was not written by him. I knew this because I'd immediately observed that the salutation was *to* him (the *O* in *Dear O.J.* containing yet another smiling face). Looking at the bottom of the second sheet—the letter's fourth page—I saw that it was signed only as *Me.*

The identity of the letter's author wasn't hard to deduce. The opening paragraph made it plain:

A Work of Fiction

I'm sorry for what happened in Vegas. Please understand that I would never *do anything to embarass you.* Ever. *Dont forget that a lot of this is still hard for me. I'm a beach girl from Orange County. I'm not used to being around celebritys. Not like you are anyway.* Please *be patient with me.*

Nicole. When had she written this? I looked at the postmark again. The year was faded, but it looked like "1980." What had happened in Vegas?

I had never met her. On the few occasions I'd ever been with Simpson before today, she'd either been separated or divorced from him. Or dead. I read the rest of the letter:

Mr. Sinatra was laughing. He thought it was funny. I know he did. Anyway, I am *older than Mia Farrow was when they got married (she was 19) so it's the truth. And I still dont think he thought I was being rude. If anything I thought he was being mean to* you *by bringing up my age.*

What hurts me is that you didn't believe me. I know I said some mean things to you at the hotel and I'm sorry for saying them. But be honest. Did you need to lock me out of the suite just for that? It was horrible. Just in my bra and panties out in the hall in the middle of the night. I couldn't even look *at the guard when he asked me what happened. And no for the 10th time I didn't say anything to him. But O.J., he let me into* your *room. He knew I was staying there. If you don't want to be embarased, maybe you should be more careful too.*

I love you and I know you love me too. Let's not do this anymore. Someday I want to be the best wife you ever had (joke!) and the only *one you ever want to have for-ever.*

Please call me when you get this.

Love,
Me

They weren't married yet. It was a sweet note, yet it revealed a side of Nicole that I'd heard people say characterized their entire relationship: her unwillingness ever to wholly capitulate to him. *Maybe you should be more careful too,* she'd told him. Even in apologizing, she wasn't prepared to completely prostrate herself to him.

I fingered the tiny cassette. Why had he written LIAR! LISTEN TO THE TAPE! on the envelope? I didn't have a microcassette player, so I wouldn't be able to find out.

Then it hit me. I did have one. My telephone answering machine used a microcassette tape to record the incoming messages. It would probably work if I just switched the tapes and pressed the message button.

Which is exactly what I did. The tape was already rewound, so I pressed *message* and waited to hear something. A long moment passed with only silence. I put my ear close to the machine, trying to hear *any* sound, however faint.

The sharp jangling of a ringing telephone made me recoil. Instinctively, I reached for my own phone, then realized the sound was coming from the tape. On the third ring, someone answered.

"Hello?"

A woman's voice.

"Hello, Nic. It's me."

Simpson.

"Hi there, you!"

Her tone sounded bright. Obviously happy to hear from him.

"I got your letter."

"Good. I'm glad."

"Why do you keep sayin' those things about me?"

He sounded harsh and hurt at the same time.

"What are you talking about, O.J.? I said I was sorry."

She seemed genuinely taken aback by his reaction.

"Stuff like I locked you out. You told me that you didn't know how you could stay with me if I didn't trust you. Leaving was your idea."

"O.J., you pushed me into the hallway."

Her voice was now flat, emotionless. They had clearly been over this before.

"Yeah, but it was your idea. You wanted to leave. You said that. Why are you lyin' about it now?"

He was on edge. Not yelling, but not far from it either.

"O.J., I said I was sorry. What more do you want from me. I'm not—"

"So you admit that I didn't lock you out? You were the

one who wanted to go and I let you go? Ain't that right?''
There was a pause, then the woman's voice came back
quiet, defeated.

"Yes. I guess that's what happened."

*"I'm glad you finally remembered it right. And next time
just keep quiet around someone like Frank Sinatra. If you
think I was pissed off, you don't know what pissed off is.
And you don't wanna know. So, when you comin' back up
here, baby? I miss you."*

In an instant his tone had totally changed. He was now
friendly, cajoling.

"I miss you, too."

This was barely audible.

*"Then get in your car. I'm takin' you out. We'll get din-
ner at Spago, then do whatever you want. A movie. A club.
You name it."*

"Okay. It'll take me a little while to get ready."

*"Baby, you can drive up naked if that'll get you here
quicker. Hey, that's a good idea. Just take off all your
clothes and jump in the car. I'll be waiting for you with
open arms. And something else, too."*

He was exuberant now.

*"Okay, O.J. Let me hang up so I can get up there,
Okay?"*

"All right, sweets. Just hurry."

"I will. Bye. I really love you."

She said these last words as if she were desperate to believe
them herself.

"I know. Me, too. Just come home."
"I will. Bye."
"Bye, sweets."

When the tape clicked off, all I could do was stare into space. God, how *awful*. And he'd *recorded* the whole thing. Why? The reason had to be so he could prove he was right and she was wrong. That she was—as he'd furiously written across the envelope—a LIAR!

The many levels of hurt they seemed capable of reaching with each other were staggering and immeasurably sad. How could he treat her like that? She was just a young woman— barely more than a girl, really—who was obviously in love with him. Yet it seemed more important to him to win their argument than to make up with her. What was the expression? *Winning isn't everything. It's the only thing.*

God rest that poor girl's soul, I thought. At least she didn't have to fight with him anymore.

Then, from downstairs, I heard a familiar voice.

"Dad?"

It was Laura.

CHAPTER SEVEN

I jumped up from the desk, threw open the office door, and ran to the top of the stairs. Looking down, I saw Laura in the entryway, holding her red raincoat, not moving. Going to the top step, I saw she was staring at Simpson, who was where I'd left him, stretched out on the couch. A pair of half glasses was perched on his nose and *The Godfather* was splayed open on his chest. He seemed a little amused by Laura's reaction to him.

She still hadn't moved. Her wet raincoat was creating a small puddle on the floor. Holding the red coat with her arms extended in front of her, she looked like a toreador who was expecting the bull to charge at any moment. As I started down the stairs she finally broke off staring at Simpson and looked up at me. Her expression was one of utter confusion.

She turned quickly back to face him, as if he might not be there should she avert her gaze from him.

The Confession of O.J. Simpson

From the couch, Simpson was the first to speak. "Hello!" he said. He knew how to use that voice to its best effect. Even in a one-word greeting, his resonant baritone conveyed tremendous warmth.

"Uh, hello?" was Laura's tentative reply. Her question was directed at me, not him.

By now I'd reached the bottom of the stairs and went directly to her. I took the wet coat from her hands. By making her release it to me, I also got her attention. My look said, *It's okay. I'll explain everything. Just go along with me on this.* I draped the coat over my left arm and, with my right arm around her, gently steered Laura into the living room.

"O.J., this is my daughter," I said.

"You're Laura, right?"

How did *he* know that? I tried to remember when I'd ever mentioned Laura by name to him. I didn't think I had.

"Right," said Laura. She wasn't normally monosyllabic, but how normal was this?

Simpson put the book down on the coffee table, removed his reading glasses, and got up off the couch. He came through the living room to the entryway and extended his hand to Laura.

Hesitating only slightly, she took it. For the first time I noticed just how big his hands were. Her small hand was completely dwarfed by his.

"It's a pleasure to meet you. You're more beautiful than your pictures." He was mellifluous.

I did understand *this* reference. My living room was filled with pictures of Laura at every age: on a pony; her middle-school

70

graduation; her sixteenth birthday party two summers ago (would she really be *eighteen* in a few months?). He'd clearly been studying them while I was upstairs . . . studying him.

"Thank you." Laura's voice was tentative. She looked at me, still hoping I might explain what was going on.

I tried. "Mr. Simpson is here on a legal matter, sweetheart. I'm reviewing some of his documents in my office. He's waiting down here until I'm done."

"Oh." She obviously wasn't satisfied with this explanation, but seemed to sense it would be pointless to ask for more details, at least not in front of him.

Instead she said, "I'd better hang that in the bathroom." She took the still-wet coat back from me and carried it into the downstairs bathroom in the rear of the house, off the kitchen.

When she'd left the room, Simpson said, "Pretty girl. How old is she?"

Something in me tightened at his question and the answer that immediately sprang to mind was, *It's none of your goddamned business*. Instead, I was truthful, if somewhat restrained. "Seventeen," I said.

"She's very pretty," he said again.

"Yes, she is. Thank you." I was terse now. Laura was not a subject I wanted on the agenda.

She came back into the room and said, "Dad, can I use your computer for a little while? I need to print something out for school and our printer isn't working. I have a disk, so it'll only take a few minutes."

"Sure, honey. Come back upstairs with me."

71

"Thanks." She said this over her shoulder, her blond hair trailing behind her. She was already halfway up the stairs.

I turned to Simpson. In a low voice, I said, "She won't stay long. Let me get back up there." I suddenly felt like a conspirator in my own house.

He said, "Fine, man. Just do what you gotta do. I know you're helping me. By the way, do you know where the remote for the TV is?"

"It's in there." I pointed at the two-doored wood cabinet underneath the television. "It's on a little shelf, above the videotapes."

"Thanks."

I turned around and started back upstairs. Then it hit me. *The book.* It was lying open on my desk and Laura was in there. Alone. I took the stairs two at a time.

When I walked back into my office, the sudden brightness forced me to squint. She'd turned on the overhead light, and for a moment I had difficulty adjusting to the glare.

"You keep it too dark in here, Dad." She was setting up at the computer table in the corner. She'd already put the chair back to where Simpson had moved it from that morning.

As I approached my desk I checked quickly to see if anything had been moved. It *looked* untouched, but it was hard to tell. And I knew my daughter. She didn't miss much.

Before I could turn around, she'd moved behind me and closed the office door. Now, facing me, she wanted some answers.

"What is he *doing* here?" She was speaking in a loud

whisper. When Laura was angry, as she was now, she bore an uncanny resemblance to her mother.

"I told you. He has me checking on some papers of his. He needs some legal advice. It's not a big deal."

"It's not a big *deal*? You let that . . . that *person* in your house and you don't think that's a big *deal*? Dad, he *murdered* two people! That *is* a big deal."

"Please keep your voice down, Laura."

"Why?" She'd lowered her voice, but I could still hear the sarcasm. "Are you afraid he'll get *mad*? Maybe turn *violent*?"

"I'm just giving him my opinion. Everyone is entitled to have access to an attorney. Even him. You know that."

"Don't try to rationalize it that way, Dad. You know there are other lawyers he can get. And you're the one who's always saying to me that one of the benefits of finally being your own boss is you get to choose what cases you want to take."

She was right. I had said that. If there'd been one consolation after the Belli debacle it was that I didn't need to engage, even tacitly, in ambulance chasing anymore. Now Laura was throwing my own argument back in my face. *She was going to be a great attorney,* I thought wryly.

"Look, Laura, I'm almost done. He won't be here long." I'd now said the same thing to each of them.

"Can you please just trust me?" I continued. "You know I only do what you tell me to do. I remember who's boss in this family." This was our standard repartee and it usually worked.

Not today. "Jesus, Dad. It's *O. J. Simpson.* Why are you even *thinking* about it?"

73

The Confession of O. J. Simpson

I had no good answer for that. Fortunately for me, that was also her last salvo. She turned on her heel and went back to the computer. In a moment her fingers were flying across the keyboard. She was still mad, but she'd finished arguing with me.

I went to my desk and started to put the yellow legal pages neatly back into the black binder.

"Are those his?" she asked.

"Yes."

"What are they?"

"Just some notes of his. Nothing important. He wants to know if . . . if they can help him with his appeal of the civil case."

She looked at me with such sadness I had to look away.

"You're helping him appeal the judgment?" She said this in complete disbelief.

"Laura, that's not what I said." I heard myself getting defensive. Not good.

I took a breath and made sure my next words were spoken evenly, without an edge in my voice.

"I'm just giving him my opinion, sweetheart. I haven't agreed to do anything more than that."

This was technically true, but irrelevant. Simpson believed that once I started reading his journal, it was understood I'd agreed to help him with his plan. And I'd done nothing to dissuade him from that view. The crushing irony of all this was if I continued to help him, it would only diminish me in my daughter's eyes. Yet I'd convinced myself that the only reason I'd gone this far was because the money I could make by helping him would be enough to pay for Laura's college. Was I really being selfless? What did that *mean,* anyway? If I was being honest with myself, wasn't sending Laura to Harvard just a vainglorious act on my part? *My* daughter, who wanted to be a lawyer like her father, would now be able to go to the most prestigious school in the nation. And all because of me. How "selfless" was that?

Laura was finished and standing in the doorway, ready to leave.

"Call Mom," she told me. "She really needs to talk to you."

"I know. I'll call her tonight. Let me walk you out."

We went downstairs. Simpson was back on the couch, watching TV. He looked up, but said nothing. It was still raining hard outside. Laura went to the front hall closet to get an umbrella.

"I'll get your coat," I said.

I walked rapidly to the back bathroom where she'd hung it up. Passing through the kitchen, I noticed there was water on the floor. I looked up. It was dripping out of a small crack in the kitchen ceiling. This part of the house was only one story, so I knew it was coming in from outside.

It never rains but it pours, I thought dryly.

I looked around the cupboards for a big pot, but couldn't find one. So I grabbed a large bowl from the counter and put it on the floor, directly under the leak. Then I grabbed Laura's coat and rushed back to her.

When I got back, she and Simpson were standing together.

The Confession of O.J. Simpson

I'd been gone no more than a minute. They both looked at me as I approached. Simpson was smiling. Laura looked pale.

"Your daughter's been telling me that she's going to Harvard. You must be very proud of her."

"I am. Here's your coat, sweetheart. I'll call you tonight."

As I handed her the coat Simpson intercepted it.

He said, "Here, let me help you with that."

He held it up for her to get into. The perfect gentleman. Awkward though it was, there was little either of us could do. She extended her arms into the coat as he draped it over her shoulders.

Quickly, she said, "Bye, Dad." A second "bye" was said in his direction when she was already out the door.

I looked angrily at Simpson.

He said, "Nice girl."

"What did you say to her?" I couldn't stop myself. I had to know.

He reacted as if he didn't know what I was talking about. "What do you mean?"

I repeated it. "I asked you what you said to her."

"Nothing, man. College, that's *all*."

"Just leave her alone, okay?" I said.

Now he was indignant. "What are you talkin' about? I didn't do anything to her. Hey, you don't believe me? I'll prove it to you."

Then, reaching into his pants pocket, he pulled out a cassette player. A *microcassette* player.

"Here. Listen to this."

A Work of Fiction

The whirr of a brief rewind was followed by voices. His voice. And Laura's voice.

Simpson: *So you must be about ready for college, right?*
Laura: *Yeah. Uh-huh.*
Simpson: *Where you gonna go?*
Laura: *Harvard. I hope . . . Harvard.*
Simpson: *Wow. That's great. There's a lot of smart guys there. I'll bet they're gonna love meeting you. You'll make 'em forget about studying for a while.*
Laura: *I guess. Whatever.*
Simpson: *Your daughter's been telling me that she's going to Harvard. You must be very proud of her.*
Then, my voice: *I am. Here's your coat, sweetheart. I'll call you tonight.*

He clicked off the tape recorder.

"See, man. I told you I didn't do *nothin'*."

I just stared at him, incredulous.

"You recorded my *daughter*?" I finally managed to say. "Why would you do something like that? What is wrong with you?"

He looked at me hard. Without a trace of apology he said, "Nothing's wrong with me, Sam. You wanna know why I keep a tape recorder in my pocket all the time now? It's because of times just like this. When I'm alone with a woman—any woman—it don't matter if she's your daughter or Princess Di, I gotta protect myself now. Anybody can say anything they want

77

about me now. And people will believe them. Remember, I'm O. J. Simpson. I'm guilty until proven innocent.''

I shook my head at this, trying to clear it. He taped *everybody* now? Laura was right. Why had I even let him in the house? We looked at each other for what seemed a very long time, neither of us speaking. He finally broke the silence.

"Hey, man, it's almost time for *Rivera Live*. You wanna order some food?''

CHAPTER EIGHT

What had I gotten myself into? It would be so simple right now to just go upstairs, get his damned book (*The Book of the Damned*?) and hand it back to him—"no harm, no foul." I'd read some embarrassing material, but nothing that actually incriminated him in any way. I wasn't yet privy to any details of what really happened on June 12 (if they were even written down, which I'd begun to doubt).

That's it, I decided. I was done with him. It wasn't worth it. All that remained was to break my decision to him.

"C'mon, Sam. Let's get something to eat and watch some tube." We were both still in the entryway. "You need a break from reading my life story. Hell, *I* need a break from *livin'* my life story."

"O.J., I don't think I can help you." *Damn me! Why had I qualified it?*

The Confession of O. J. Simpson

"What? Why not?" He seemed genuinely surprised. And hurt.

"I just . . . I've read a lot of the material . . . your notes from the trial, some correspondence . . . and . . . it's *interesting*. . . . I suppose it will make a compelling book or a movie . . . but there's nothing in there . . . I mean, what you asked me . . . anyone could . . ."

I couldn't believe what I was doing. Instead of telling him straight out, "I'm sorry, I just don't want to be involved with this," I was hemming and hawing about how the "material" wasn't right. Like some actor complaining about a script.

Simpson sensed that my "decision" wasn't final. And he immediately tried to target my weak points.

"Listen, Sam. I *know* I'm not your most favorite person in the world. And I could tell your daughter didn't think much of me neither. But what am I supposed to *do,* man? Am I not allowed to support my kids? You love your girl, don't you? What if somebody said you weren't allowed to take care of her anymore? How would you feel, Sam?"

Bull's-eye.

"The jury said I wasn't guilty. That's supposed to mean somethin' in this country. I'm an American. I'm a *good* American. Where do they want us to go? Back to Africa?"

I was wavering. What was wrong with me?

I tried to rally. "O.J., this just seems like a waste of time for both of us. Like I said to you at the outset, you need a writer, not a lawyer. There's nothing in those pages that's incriminating. At least nothing I've read so far. If you want to make up a confession for Goldman, just get someone to help you write it yourself.''

"Sam, there's more stuff there that you ain't read yet. And here's the thing, man. I don't trust nobody else.''

"O.J., that's nice to hear, but you hardly know me. What makes you think I'm the only person you can trust to do this?''

"You may not be the only one, Sam. But you're the one I want. You wanna know why I come to you? I'll tell you. You know that time you were at my house, a few years ago, whenever it was?''

I nodded.

"You were workin' for Belli. And somebody, I don't know who it was, maybe Howard Weitzman, talked some trash about Belli. Like 'that old crook,' or some shit like that. You could've let it pass. I remember thinkin' that. But you didn't. You talked right up and said, 'I'd appreciate it if you didn't speak about my colleague that way.' That's what you said. Stopped the conversation dead, but I thought *damn,* this guy's got balls. And he's loyal. Do you remember that?''

I did have a vague memory of the conversation. The problem was there'd been so *many* times when I'd had to defend Belli in public, it was virtually impossible to separate them in my memory.

There was some cruel symmetry to all this. He'd remembered me because I'd been loyal to Belli, who, as it turned out, *was* a crook who'd stolen everything I had. Now the reason I was even considering helping Simpson was because Belli had made it necessary for me to do so.

The Confession of O.J. Simpson

I looked at him and thought, *Oh Christ, I've gone this far. Why not?*

What I said was, "There's a Chinese menu in the kitchen."

He grinned.

We started walking toward the kitchen and I brought up something that had been nagging at me.

"When you met my daughter, you already knew her name. How was that? I don't think I'd said it to you before."

"No, you didn't say it to me. I heard your ex-wife say it on the phone upstairs. Don't you remember? You owe them a couple of checks. . . ."

I flushed at his casual mention of my personal affairs. On the other hand, perhaps it was only fair that while I was reading his private thoughts, he'd been carefully studying me as well.

"Here's the menu. Pick out what you want and I'll call it in."

"What are you gonna have?"

"I don't know. I usually get the cashew chicken, that's good. Sometimes a beef dish. Beef with scallions."

"That sounds great. Go for it. Just make it a double order of both those things."

"That's a lot of food. Are you sure—" I stopped myself. He'd probably try to eat my portion anyway. While I placed the order from the phone in the kitchen, he went back out to the living room and turned on the television. After I'd hung up with the restaurant, I joined him.

"They said with the rain and all it might take as long as an hour."

"That's okay. Hey, Sam. Take a look at this."

He was on the couch with the remote in his hand. His feet were propped up on the coffee table. I sat down next to him.

He was watching MTV. The video featured a bawdy-looking blond woman who I thought I recognized as Madonna.

"Hey, check her out, man. She's *hot.*"

"Isn't that Madonna?"

He shot me a look like I was from another planet.

"Sam. Where you *been,* man? That's that Love chick. Courtney Love. You know, she was married to that dude who shot himself. That Nirvana guy. What's his name. Cocaine. Kurt Cocaine. You know who I'm talkin' about, don't ya?"

He obviously didn't expect an answer, because he'd already changed the channel—cutting Courtney Love off in mid-yowl.

"She's fine, but she can't sing worth shit. Hey, look, it's my *man.*"

It was Johnnie Cochran's show on Court TV. Al Gore was his guest.

"See what I was sayin'? Johnnie's a star, man. He's a fuckin' hero now. And *I* made him. It's all because of *me. Marcia*"—he drawled the name—"she didn't get her show, did she?"

He'd hit *mute* before either Cochran or Gore could get out a word. Then he switched channels again.

Golf.

"Wait a minute . . . here we go. I don't know what tournament this is . . . let's see if they show the leader board. . . . Hey, Sam! Look at that! My boy's doin' it *again*! He's no tiger, he's a *lion*! And he's roarin' now, Sam! Will you look at that? He's up by *eleven* strokes. Eleven fucking *strokes*! Just look at him putting here. . . ."

He was sitting up now. His shoulders were hunched and he was leaning forward over the coffee table, as close as he could get to the screen. It was as if he, not Tiger Woods, was lining up to putt.

A silent moment passed and then Tiger stroked the ball. It traveled on a wide arc for about twenty feet and then curved back toward the flag until it dropped, dead center, into the hole.

"Yes!" He pumped his fist into the air. Anyone would have believed he'd sunk the putt himself. On the screen, Woods's own reaction was significantly more subdued. He picked up the ball, smiled, and waved at the large crowd that followed him from hole to hole. Then he walked toward the next tee.

"Sam, I'm so proud of him. He's doin' *exactly* what I told him he should do."

I was surprised. "You know him?"

"Sure. Well, I mean we know the same people. I've called him on the phone a few times. He's got some real assholes workin' for him, though. They never let him talk to me. But I know he's been getting my messages. I can tell he gets 'em, because he's been doin' exactly what I said he should do."

"Like what?"

"Like everything, man. See how he always smiles when he finishes a hole? I told him he had to do that, because the camera's always on him then. See that wave he does to the crowd?

84

A Work of Fiction

You ever see me when I'm at an event or anything, I *always* wave. I'm telling you, people, they *notice* that shit.''

"He's certainly got a lot of poise for his age," I ventured neutrally.

"Damn right he does. Just like me. I was the same way when I won my Heisman. Hell, I was *younger* than him. 'Young, dumb, and full of cum,' you know what I'm sayin'? We're so much *alike,* man. You know he had the biggest audience ever for golf when he won his Masters—it was somethin' like forty-four, forty-five million people. Let me tell you something, Sam, I had more than *twice* that much in the Bronco. I got ninety-five million. Think about that. *Ninety-five million.* You got anything to drink?''

"There's some more Coke in the fridge." I started to get up.

He put his hand on my arm. "No, I mean anything to *drink.* You got any of the good stuff?''

I rarely drank, but I did have a few bottles of wine and hard liquor that a few of my clients had given me as gifts.

"I can check. What do you like?''

"See if you have any Scotch. That would be great. Straight up." He was mesmerized by Tiger's latest drive, which the announcers seemed to think had traveled farther than was humanly possible.

"Look at that drive, Sam. You know what they say: 'drive for show, putt for dough.' My boy can do it *all,* I'm tellin ya, man. . . .''

I got up and went to the front hall closet. The top shelf

doubled as my liquor cabinet. I found a bottle of Johnnie Walker, which I took down and brought out to the kitchen. I picked up the bowl of rainwater and emptied it into the sink. Looking up at the ceiling, I noticed the leak had stopped. It also wasn't raining anymore. I took a clean glass from the dish drainer and poured him a drink. Then I thought, *If not now, when?*—and poured a small one for myself.

When I got back to the living room, Tiger was putting again. I knew this because Simpson was leaning so close to the screen, he was almost *in* the television. I put his drink down on the table and sat down just as the ball stopped rolling. It was a few inches shy of the hole.

"Damn. That was for eagle." He grabbed the drink and took a large swallow. I took a sip of mine.

The golf broadcast had gone to a commercial and he immediately started channel surfing again. He stopped back on MTV, and Courtney Love had, by now, given way to someone else. A rapper.

Suddenly he was shouting at the screen. "Fuck you, *motherfucker*! Fuck *you* and your rap fucking shit song."

He was totally out of control and I had no idea why. The video was just ending and the title flashed in the corner of the screen. It was called "I Used to Love Her," and it was by someone apparently named "Ice-T."

He switched back to golf.

"What was that all about?"

"What was what?"

He said this distractedly, his attention entirely focused on the TV screen. It didn't even seem to register that I was talking to him.

This was too strange to let pass. "How come you were shouting at the television?"

He glanced at me. "Oh, just some motherfucker wrote this song about me and Nicole. Said I was guilty and walkin' around playin' golf. Who gives a shit?"

Simpson was now completely engrossed in the golf match again, as if nothing had happened. In a few seconds he'd put the whole thing out of his mind. He could turn on a dime.

"Didn't you say you wanted to watch Geraldo?"

I had his attention again. This was potentially about *him.* "Oh, right. What time is it?"

I checked my watch. "A little after six," I said.

"Shit, he goes on at six." He switched channels rapidly until he found CNBC.

"We're back. Our guest tonight is former Los Angeles police detective—and admitted perjurer—Mark Fuhrman, whose best-selling book, Murder in Brentwood, *is just out in paperback. Mark, thank you for joining us tonight."*

"You're welcome, Geraldo."

"You know, Geraldo should send me a check every week. He's been doin' me for years now and it still gets him ratings. Did you know during my first trial, he had the highest ratings in the history of CNBC?"

I said I hadn't known that.

The Confession of O. J. Simpson

"Mark, a while back we had you and Alan Dershowitz on the program, you were on the phone, and he called you ... let me find the quote ... 'a charming fascist.' How's your charm holding up?"
"Better than his, I think."

Simpson laughed uproariously at this. "You tell 'em, Mark!" he said to the screen.

"Do we have some of that videotape. We do. Okay, here's Professor Dershowitz on the subject of Mark Fuhrman."

"You're lying to the American public. Those were not the statements of somebody making a screenplay. They were the statements of a vicious, racist, sexist miserable cop who the American public is falling for because you're a charming fascist. That is what you are, a charming fascist."

"He clearly has some strong feelings about you, Mark. Does it bother you that you're still such a lightning rod for people?"
"You know, Geraldo, I've always believed you can tell a lot about someone by who their enemies are. And if Alan Dershowitz hates me, then I'm doin' all right."
"Do you consider O. J. Simpson your enemy?"
"I don't consider O. J. Simpson at all."

"Fuck *you,* you lying piece of shit!" He hit the mute button and turned to me, seething. His features were totally contorted. He looked like a different person.

"I had that bastard in my *house.* He 'don't consider me.' Like hell he don't. He considered me well enough when he was soakin' in my fuckin' hot tub, I can tell you that."

"What are you talking about?" He'd lost me completely.

He was calmer now, but only slightly. He downed the last of his drink in one swallow.

"I knew Fuhrman. I knew him, man. *Before.* He came out to my house years ago when me and Nicole had a beef. Nothing happened, no report or nothin', we was just arguing and I accidentally broke the windshield of her car. It was *my* car, really . . . it was in *my* name. Anyway, I invited him over to the house and he came by two, maybe three weeks later. He loved it. Hangin' with The Juice, you know what I'm sayin'?"

I thought I did. "This never came out at the trial, did it?"

"You mean that I knew him before?"

"Right."

"No, why should it have? I mean, think about it, Sam. If he says he's been to my house not on police business, then he can't be a witness. And he wanted to be a witness so bad. He wanted to be the big man. He found the glove. Remember what he said on the tape: 'Without me, there's no case.' He couldn't tell nobody, 'cuz then for sure the DA couldn't use him."

"Didn't anybody else know? And how come your attorneys didn't use it?"

"Why would we? We *wanted* him to testify. We knew from

the start that he was gonna be our 'Simi Valley' guy. Good as gold.''

This was all hard to absorb. Why wouldn't Fuhrman have come forward now and used this as absolute proof he never would have framed Simpson? If they'd been social friends, then he . . . oh, *that* was it. He could never talk about it, even now, because something happened with Simpson that he didn't want anyone to know about.

I had a pretty good guess what it was, too. Fuhrman was probably going to file a report that day and he got talked out of it by someone even more "charming" than he was. A phrase from the trial—I don't remember who said it—popped into my head: "He can always 'O.J.' his way out of anything." That's probably what happened. "Come on back to the house, man. You'll take a swim. We'll have some barbecue. It'll be great.'' No harm, no foul.

Now both of them had good reason never to mention it. Fuhrman's book wouldn't have quite the same cachet if it turned out he and Simpson were old hot-tub buddies. And Simpson's ongoing civil appeals would lose the card they kept trying to play—their ace in the hole—Mark Fuhrman, rogue cop and un-repentant racist.

"So," I said, "what's he like?''

He was watching golf again, so I knew I was about to lose him.

"Who? Oh, Fuhrman. He's okay. Tells good jokes. *C'mon,* why would you use an *iron,* for chrissakes." He and Tiger were communing again.

A Work of Fiction

It was time for me to get back upstairs, but I needed to talk to him first. I waited until the next commercial break, when I knew I could get his full attention. When it came, I took the remote from his hand and pressed *mute* myself.

"O.J., if you don't want to be here all night, I need to ask you something."

He was looking directly at me now. He wanted the remote back.

"Sure. Go ahead."

"I mentioned to you before that there wasn't anything incriminating in the papers I've read so far. I guess I need to ask you . . . is there anything you've written about . . . about that night?"

He looked at me closely before answering. "You want to know what happened, right?"

"Isn't that why you have me reading this?"

"All right. Here's what you need to read. There's an envelope—it's got a red mark on the front that says it's personal—it's addressed to me. You read that. It'll tell you all about what happened between me and Nicole."

If he'd been a witness I was cross-examining, I'd have said, "But Mr. Simpson, you haven't answered my question. I didn't ask you anything about your relationship with Nicole." However, he wasn't my witness. He was—there was no getting away from it now—my client.

"Okay," I exhaled, tired now. "If you say so. Let me get back at it, then. Just let me know when the food gets here, will you?" I handed him back the remote.

"I will." He was switching channels yet again. He had a very short attention span.

Getting up from the couch, I had a brief moment of vertigo. I really wasn't used to drinking. He didn't even notice. It took a second to pass, then I walked with precision over to the stairs. Turning back to look at him, I saw what he was watching now: *Jeopardy!*

"I'll take Movies for two hundred, Alex."
"And the Double Jeopardy answer is: 'This actress played legendary screenstar Norma Desmond in the 1950 film classic Sunset Boulevard.' "

"Oh, man. I *know* this! Who was . . . who was . . . oh, I *got* it! Who was *Glenn Close!*"

I went upstairs.

CHAPTER NINE

The envelope was easy to find. It had been stamped both PERSONAL *and* CONFIDENTIAL in red letters below the address. The letter had been sent to *Mr. Orenthal J. Simpson* in care of his Orenthal Enterprises on San Vicente Boulevard in Los Angeles.

I opened it and removed several pages of what appeared to be a typewritten memorandum of some kind. Once I found my reading glasses, I was able to see that it was dated June 4, 1994. It was single-spaced and covered both sides of eight pages. The first page indicated it was a memo to Simpson. It read:

To: OJS
From: MEB
Re: Subject Movements: 5/21–6/4
Date: 6/5/94

The Confession of O.J. Simpson

On 5/21 Subject Nicole Simpson was initially observed outside 875 Bundy Drive residence at 0630 hours. At 0631 hours Subject reenters residence with newspaper. At 0850 hours Subject and two minor children (Sydney Simpson and Justin Simpson) depart residence via rear garage. Subject and children proceed in Subject's vehicle west on Dorothy Street. Surveillance continued en route. At 0859 hours Subject and minor children arrive at Elementary School in Santa Monica. Subject escorts children into school. At 0905 hours Subject reenters vehicle and proceeds north on 23rd St.. Surveillance continued en route. At 0915 hours Subject reenters Bundy Drive residence via rear garage. At 0916 hours telephonic surveillance engaged. Transcription follows.

Unidentified Female:	hello?
Subject:	hi.
Unidentified Female:	hi.
Subject:	are you ready?
Unidentified Female:	i can be. how is ten minutes at the corner?
Subject:	9:30?
Unidentified Female:	perfect.
Subject:	bye.
Unidentified Female:	bye.

Telephonic surveillance terminated at 0917 hours. At 0927 hours Subject departs residence via Bundy Drive. Subject proceeds north on Bundy Drive on foot. Surveillance continued en route. At 0932 hours Subject meets unidentified female (description: blond, approximately five foot six inches in height, approximately one hundred twenty to one hundred thirty pounds in weight, approximately thirty to thirty-five years of age) on northwest corner of San Vicente Boulevard and Bundy Drive. At 0933 hours Subject and unidentified female begin running west on San

94

A Work of Fiction

Vicente Boulevard. Surveillance continued en route. Subject and unidentified female observed running west on the north side of San Vicente Boulevard to Ocean Avenue, then crossing San Vicente, continue running east on the south side of San Vicente Boulevard. At 1041 hours Subject and unidentified female terminate run at southwest corner of San Vicente Boulevard and Bundy Drive. At 1047 hours Subject reenters Bundy residence.

He was having her followed by a private investigator. From the looks of this, possibly more than one. And her telephone was tapped. My immediate reaction was that no one in his right mind would go that far. Then, of course, I realized where that thinking inevitably led. And I didn't want to go there.

Flipping through the pages, looking for anything that might be significant, I remained skeptical, thinking this was yet another exercise in futility (the report covered a period that ended eight days *prior* to June 12, which ruled out an eyewitness account of the murders). Still, he'd been so insistent that this memo would "answer all your questions," I was willing to skim through it on the off chance he *was* telling the truth. I'd also begun to realize his idea of "the truth" was different from mine or most people's. For Simpson, truth was something for other people to believe *when he* told it to them. The more persuasive he was, the "truer" something could be.

I noticed that a few of the transcripts of telephone conversations had been overscored with a yellow highlighter pen. This seemed unlike something he would have had the patience to do himself. I wondered if anyone else had reviewed this report for him.

The Confession of O.J. Simpson

One of the yellow-marked conversations was dated "5/22." It read:

At 12:10 hours telephonic surveillance engaged. Transcription follows.

Unidentified Female:	hello?
Subject:	well i did it.
Unidentified Female:	nicole?
Subject:	i really did it this time. i gave him back the bracelet and the diamond earrings too. that's it faye. it's over. can you believe it? it's really over.

(Note: unidentified female is now presumed to be Faye Resnick, friend of Subject.)

Resnick:	slow down. what are you telling me? you gave them back to o.j.?
Subject:	he wasn't happy. but he didn't lose it either. he was funny even. he said i've been expecting this. it's that time of month.
Resnick:	god more of that pms crap.
Subject:	no he didn't go off on that. it was a little strange. he sounded i don't know he sounded relieved i guess.
Resnick:	he must have paula back.

A Work of Fiction

Subject: don't know. maybe. look he wasn't happy for me or anything. i'm not saying that.

Resnick: that would be a little too much to ask nic.

Subject: yeah. but anyway i did it. it feels so amazing. like my head is clear for the first time since i got sick. maybe for the first time period.

Resnick: i hear you. let's have lunch. we have to celebrate. you're a free woman.

Subject: not so free. he's not going to make it easy with money. he already said that. he said if i don't want to be with him i have to start paying my own way.

Resnick: he still wants control.

Subject: faye he is right in a way. i can't run to him for money if i get in trouble. i have to change that.

Resnick: but they are his children too. don't forget that you have a full time job even if it doesn't pay a salary. he has to understand that.

Subject: he does.

Resnick: anyway don't worry about money today. today is my treat. and tonight we are going out. this is a red letter day. mark it down on your calendar girl. it's your own fourth of july.

Subject: you're funny. thank you for being my friend. really.

The Confession of O.J. Simpson

Resnick: who else could i be? where do you want to have lunch. mezzaluna? does that cute boy work daytime?

Subject: no he's only on nights. but we can go there anyway. he sometimes comes by. there or starbucks.

Resnick: do you want to say one o'clock?

Subject: sure. i'll meet you there.

Resnick: bring that blouse you want to take back. we can do some shopping after.

Subject: i've got to pick up the kids at three.

Resnick: bring it anyway in case.

Subject: ok. bye.

Resnick: bye.

Telephonic surveillance terminated at 1213 hours.

I could see why this section had been highlighted. Nicole had finally ended her relationship with Simpson. This was his chance to hear exactly what she would tell her friends about the breakup. Did he still want her back? Or was Nicole's perception accurate when she'd said he sounded "relieved"? It was interesting to me that the issue of money had come up so quickly. I guess it always did. (God, I *had* to call Rachel tonight.) On the other hand, I thought there was something extraordinarily cynical about him putting financial pressure on the mother of his children

when he was spending what literally had to be thousands of
dollars to have her spied on day and night.

There still wasn't anything really new here, though. It had
been public knowledge—I remembered reading about it during
one of the trials—that Nicole had broken off their reconciliation
attempt shortly before she was killed. What was he trying to
show me by having me read this? That he had a motive? This
wasn't a revelation to me, and I had barely followed the case.

The next highlighted section was a short conversation on
page seven of the investigator's report. It was between Nicole
and an "unidentified male" on May 30:

At 1637 hours telephonic surveillance engaged. Transcription
follows.

Subject:	hello?
Unidentified Male:	hi nicole it's ron goldman.
Subject:	hi. how are you?

(*Note: unidentified male is now presumed to be Ronald
Goldman, friend of Subject.*)

Goldman:	great. how you doing?
Subject:	i'm really good. really good.
Goldman:	that's terrific. how are the kids?
Subject:	they're fine. sydney has a dance recital in a couple of weeks and she's really excited. justin is at his dad's.

Goldman:	are you coming over to watch tonight? it's at jeff's.
Subject:	oh god it is monday. i can't tonight. will you tape it for me. my vcr isn't working right.
Goldman:	sure. no problem.
Subject:	what are you doing tomorrow night?
Goldman:	i have to work. why?
Subject:	i thought if you didn't mind watching it again you could come over and we could have melrose tuesday.
Goldman:	that sounds great. maybe i can switch with someone. can i call you back later?
Subject:	please do.
Goldman:	i will. all right i'll call you later then.
Subject:	ok ron. have fun tonight without me.
Goldman:	we'll try but it will be hard. bye.
Subject:	bye.

Telephonic surveillance terminated at 1640 hours.

This was interesting, but still nothing major. She'd spoken to Ron Goldman on the telephone and it seemed innocent enough. He clearly wasn't that friendly with her; at least not yet. He'd even used his surname in identifying himself to her: *"Hi, Nicole. It's Ron Goldman."* You *could* read between the lines, perhaps. She was feeling newly single again and was inviting him over to watch TV. (Didn't these people do anything else besides watch television?) Obviously, Goldman's call had some meaning to Simpson. What was interesting to me was whether or not this passage had been highlighted *before* June 12. That would speak to some specific knowledge Simpson might have had before that night about Nicole's interest, however slight, in Ron Goldman.

This was getting me nowhere. I'd learned nothing of relevance to the task I'd ostensibly been asked to perform. I stopped reading and thought for a moment. He must have had a reason for wanting me to read this report. Of course, I could go downstairs and ask him directly, but I'd had enough of him just now. I'd rather try to make sense of this without his help. Rachel would have seen this as a classic case of my stubbornness coming to the fore. ("You know how it is with you, don't you, Sam? The shortest distance between two points can't ever be just a straight line. Especially if you didn't draw the line yourself.")

So what *was* I supposed to discover here? There was no smoking gun—no *glove*—in these pages, or, for that matter, in anything I'd read so far.

I started to put the report back in the envelope, then I noticed there was one more section that he (or someone) had marked. It was the back side of the last page. That entire page had been overscored with yellow.

The date was June 4, the last day covered by the report. This section was slightly different from the others I'd read. It began with an underlined notation in capital letters:

101

The Confession of O.J. Simpson

Telephonic surveillance engaged at 1332 hours. Transcription
follows.

Unidentified Female:	hello?
Subject:	hi it's me.
Unidentified Female:	hi. you sure got home quick.
Subject:	after that i felt like I could fly under my own power.
Unidentified Female:	you guys were having quite a time up there.
Subject:	thank you so much for letting us use your place. it was the only way i knew we would be alone.
Unidentified Female:	you don't really think he's having you followed?
Subject:	i don't know. sometimes i'm sure of it then other times i think i'm just being paranoid.
Unidentified Female:	are the kids home yet?
Subject:	they went swimming at o.j.'s after school.
Unidentified Female:	is he in town?

Subject:	no. i don't think he gets back until tomorrow.
Unidentified Female:	you better hope he didn't change his plans. god nicole if he finds out.
Subject:	he won't. we're both being very careful this time.
Unidentified Female:	how did marcus get out of the house?

(Note: person under discussion presumed to be Marcus Allen. Client immediately notified per standing instructions regarding priority list.)

Subject:	he's supposed to be at an autograph show all day.
Unidentified Female:	so what did he do? sign a bunch of footballs in a hurry and then run out?
Subject:	something like that. it was so great.
Unidentified Female:	here we go again.
Subject:	he is bigger than o.j. i swear. i didn't think anyone was. he is.
Unidentified Female:	where have I heard this before?
Subject:	i told him when we were in cabo that we compared him to a piece of driftwood.
Unidentified Female:	how did he take that news?

The Confession of O.J. Simpson

Subject:	he laughed. he said he loved me too.
Unidentified Female:	oh god he said that? what did you say?
Subject:	what do you think?
Unidentified Female:	i think you're both crazy. but i'm happy for you. you know that if o.j. finds out he'll kill me for letting you use my place.
Subject:	don't worry. he won't find out.
Unidentified Female:	there goes my other line. i'll call you right back. bye.
Subject:	bye.

Telephonic surveillance terminated at 1337 hours.

This was far more serious than anything I'd read previously because it meant Simpson absolutely knew Nicole was having an affair with Marcus Allen. And apparently not for the first time either. ("We're both being very careful this time.") Even not having followed the trials closely, I knew how dangerous this was. Being a football fan, I knew Marcus Allen had always been Simpson's protégé. They both went to USC. They both won the Heisman Trophy. Allen had been almost as big a star in the NFL as Simpson. And it was common knowledge to people who followed football that they were close friends off the field as well. I vaguely remembered Allen's name having come up during one of the trials. Had he given a deposition in the civil trial? I wasn't sure. What I did know was this was pretty incendiary stuff, especially if it was being sent directly to a man with a history of jealous rages.

And he didn't even have to wait for it to come in the mail.

Imagine the reaction of the client who had left "standing instructions to be notified upon arrival of male visitor" when he got *this* phone call: "Mr. Simpson, sorry to have to tell you this, sir, but Marcus Allen is apparently having an affair with your ex-wife. Mr. Simpson? Hello?"

For the first time I felt I was beginning to understand why he wanted me to read his journal. It wasn't about any one thing. It was about *everything*. He wanted me to get inside his head. He didn't know how to tell me this was what he wanted—that would require too much self-awareness on his part. Both of which, for him, seemed to be in very short supply. He wanted me to figure him out by myself—without his help.

I looked up at the doorway and was startled to see Simpson standing right there. He'd been watching me. For how long?

He spoke before I could.

"The food's here, man. He can't break a hundred. You got anything smaller?"

CHAPTER TEN

The Chinese deliveryman was standing in the doorway. Even though it had stopped raining, he wore a slicker over his head. He didn't seem to recognize Simpson, but he *was* highly agitated about the hundred-dollar bill.

"No change. No change. You got to call first for change."

I said, "It's okay. I've got smaller bills. How much is it?"

He handed me the bill. Lots of Chinese characters with a numerical figure circled at the bottom: $37.90.

I gave him two twenties, then fished two more singles out of my pocket. He handed me the food. Crisis averted.

While I was paying the man Simpson had walked outside to his car. Now, as he came back up the walk, I saw he was holding a videotape.

"I gotta show you this," was all he said.

I headed toward the kitchen for bowls and utensils, but

The Confession of O.J. Simpson

Simpson grabbed the bag from me and took it straight into the living room.

"Don't you want that in a bowl?" I asked.

"Don't need it." He was taking all the little white cartons out of the bag and putting them on the coffee table.

"Guess Who's Coming to Dinner," I thought to myself as I watched him setting up.

"There's chopsticks in here. Get a fork if you need one, I can use these. And grab some Cokes, too, will ya?"

Actually, it was beginning to feel more like *The Man Who Came to Dinner*—the movie where the guest never leaves.

In the short time it took me to get the drinks (and a fork for myself; I *couldn't* use chopsticks), he'd already started eating out of one of the open containers. He'd also started the video-tape. Once again, I found myself on the couch watching television with him.

What we were seeing was clearly a home video. It took me only a second to recognize where it was shot: his house on Rockingham. Some sort of party was going on.

"What is this we're watching?" I asked, taking one of the cartons from him. He'd already finished one and was working on the second.

"Just keep looking. You'll see." He was staring intently at the screen.

A lot of well-dressed people with drinks in their hands were milling about, laughing and chatting. Abruptly, the tape jumped to someone talking directly into the camera. He looked familiar.

"Hey, Marcus," said the man to the camera. *"I want to*

wish you two the very best of happiness. You deserve it. You're the greatest.''

"Who's that?" I asked.

"A.C."

Oh, right. *That* was his friend Al Cowlings. I'd seen him on the news.

After several more talking heads had sent their best wishes to "Marcus" or to "the happy couple," it was easy to figure out this was Marcus Allen's wedding reception.

"Did he get married at your house?"

"Damn right, he did. In *my* fuckin' house."

"When was this?"

"Ninety-three."

A year before Nicole was killed. I noted it was also the year *prior* to the time when those surveillance tapes were made.

"Watch. Watch this lyin' motherfucker." He turned up the volume.

"O.J., I don't know what to say to you. You made this day possible. We are so grateful to you. It's something neither of us will ever forget. Thank you. I love you, bro."

Marcus Allen.

Simpson paused the tape. Allen's face froze on the screen. His mouth was open and his eyes were half-closed. He'd been trapped in a particularly unattractive frame. Knowing I fully understood why Allen's words would be so incredibly galling to him, Simpson looked to me for sympathy.

I didn't give him any. Instead, I asked him, "Were you and Nicole married when he was seeing her?"

"No, man. But we was tryin' to get back together. He knew that, too."

"But Nicole says in that report she'd already told you she didn't want to see you again. She gave you back some jewelry . . . ?"

"Oh *man,* she was always goin' back and forth like that. One day she loved me, the next day it was like she didn't know who I was. That don't mean nothing with Nicole." His right knee was pumping up and down rapidly as he spoke.

I hesitated before asking him the next question.

"O.J. . . . you said that the letter, that report to you, would answer all my questions about . . . about the murders. Did you mean that you killed Nicole because she was having an affair with Marcus Allen?"

I'd finally asked him. There was no taking it back now.

He looked at me. The mask had returned the moment he'd heard my question.

Although I was sitting less than two feet away from him, I didn't look away. I knew the moment I did, he would pretend that I'd never spoken.

Eventually he had to say something.

"I *could* tell you, Sam. But then I'd have to kill you." The mask split open into a big smile and he threw his arm around me. "Don't be so *serious,* man. We're just watchin' TV."

I stared at him for a moment, then shook my head in disbelief. I stood up, which forced him to remove his arm from my shoulder. So my abrupt movement wouldn't seem quite so harsh, I also started collecting the empty cartons of food.

A Work of Fiction

"O.J., if you don't want to tell me what happened, that's fine. But then you really are wasting my time. I can't help you if you don't level with me."

"Listen, man. I'm *telling* you everything. Really. You've been reading stuff I showed to no one but you. I told you that."

"You also told me it would contain the information necessary to prepare a confession. I've seen nothing which resembles that." I started toward the kitchen.

He got up and followed me. As I was putting the cartons in the trash, he said "Not everything's written down. Some of it I just need to tell you."

I looked at him. It was now about nine o'clock. I was already spent from the entire day. My neck hurt and I was developing a throbbing headache behind my left eye.

"When had you planned to start doing that?" I made no effort to conceal the irritation in my voice.

"Now. Right now. Just let me go to the john. Where is it? Back here?"

I nodded and pointed at the door just behind him. When he closed the door, I wondered if I really had the stamina for any more of him tonight.

I thought a moment, then decided to go upstairs and get the legal pad marked *Simpson Confession* from my desk. It seemed that I might finally need it.

A few minutes later we met back in the living room.

He was animated. Talking rapidly.

"Sam? Hey, *Sam,* I just thought of something. If I do publish this stuff, do I get to keep any of the money? Who was that guy in New York? That guy who killed all those people? Didn't they take all *his* money?''

''The Son of Sam,'' I said, smiling slightly.

''Yeah, right, the Son of Sam.'' Then the double meaning dawned on him and he returned the smile. ''No relation, right?''

''None at all,'' I said. ''As for you keeping the profits from the sale of any book or motion-picture rights, you don't have to worry about that. The Supreme Court—I think it was in ninety-one—threw out the original law which said a criminal cannot profit from his or her crime. That's the one you're talking about. I'm not sure it would even apply to you anyway, given that you were acquitted.''

While I'd been speaking, he'd been pacing nervously. His hands were in his pockets and he was jangling keys or change as he walked around the room.

I was in the chair with the legal pad and pen in my lap.

''Where do you want to begin?'' I asked.

He looked over at me, and before he could respond, his body shuddered and he sneezed violently. He tried to cover himself, but he wasn't fast enough. The front of his shirt was now covered with blood.

I bolted out of the chair and went to him. ''Are you all right?''

He was holding his nose and had his head tilted back at a horizontal angle to try to stop the bleeding. I helped him down onto the couch.

Through his hand he said, ''I'm sorry, man. You got a paper towel or somethin'?''

I grabbed a handful of towels from the kitchen and brought them to him.

"Thanks, Sam. I get these nosebleeds sometimes . . . pain in the ass." He continued to hold his head back and he was dabbing gently at his nose with the towels. While doing this he was able to see that his shirtfront was totally stained with blood. Amazingly, he'd somehow managed to get none of it on my carpet.

"Goddammit, I *like* this shirt," he said.

I said, "Let me see what I have upstairs." We were about the same height, but he was much thicker in the upper body than I was. I didn't know if I'd have anything that would fit him.

I went upstairs and rummaged through my drawers. I found a T-shirt, XXL, that I'd brought back from a political event. It said CLINTON-GORE on the front in bold letters. I chuckled to myself and brought it down to him.

His head was still tilted back, but the paper towels were now crumpled in a ball on the coffee table. The bleeding had stopped. I handed him the shirt.

"Shit! Is this *all* you've got?" His eyes made it clear that he wasn't really *asking* for another shirt. He was just going through the motions of not being willing to wear it.

I went along. "That's all I've got that will fit you. If you don't like it, you're out of luck." I was looking forward to making him put it on.

He pulled the polo shirt up over his head and stood, for a moment, bare-chested in front of me. The years had taken their toll, although not entirely. He was still well built, but his arms and upper body had definitely thickened. Surprisingly, his waist remained comparatively trim. He reminded me of some of the pictures I'd seen of heavyweight fighters just past their prime: Joe Louis, maybe Sonny Liston. Not yet George Foreman.

With a grimace, he took the T-shirt from me and put it on. It was a snug fit, but he could wear it. He looked at the blood-stained shirt in his hand and said, "I've gotta put some water on this." He went back out to the kitchen and I followed. Instead of stopping at the kitchen sink as I expected him to, he kept on going into the bathroom. He closed the door behind him.

I thought this was strange, but then again, what wasn't strange about today?

As I stood awkwardly in the kitchen waiting for him to come out, the bathroom door slowly creaked opened. The door was warped, and unless it was pulled tightly shut, it didn't close very well. Standing where I was, I suddenly found myself with a clear view of Simpson. He was crouched on the bathroom floor, his head positioned just over the sink. The bloody shirt was on the floor next to him. His face was just above the edge of the sink, and he had what appeared to be a rolled-up dollar bill stuck in his left nostril. In one motion, he inhaled whatever was on the sink and threw his head as far back as it would go, virtually perpendicular to his shoulders. He made a short guttural noise that sounded like "Aaaach!" and then he quickly straightened up. As he did so he saw me looking at him through the open door. Our eyes locked.

We both stood there for a moment, then, without speaking, he picked the bloody shirt off the floor and walked out of the bathroom.

"Sam . . ." he began.

I didn't let him finish the sentence. I spoke quietly and slowly, choosing my words carefully. I emphasized each one, as if speaking to a small child or a very slow-witted person.

"You are a guest in my house. You've asked me to represent you. What you just did is a crime. It's a felony. Maybe that doesn't mean anything to you anymore—I suppose it doesn't—but it does mean something to me when you do it in my house. Do you understand what I'm saying?"

"Yes." His head was down. For once, he couldn't look at me.

"Was that cocaine?" I already knew the answer.

"Uh-huh."

"Did you use it all up?"

He looked up at me quizzically, as if to say, *Why? Do you want some?*

Then he realized why I was asking. "Yeah. That was the last of it."

"So you have no additional drugs remaining on you now?"

"No."

I studied his face when he said this. He *appeared* to be telling the truth. But in his case, the value of appearances had long ago been established.

I walked out of the kitchen. I intended to go upstairs, gather all his papers, and hand them back to him. Before I reached the stairs, I heard him cry out. It was a keening sound, almost a wail.

"I got *nobody*! There's nobody *left*!"

The Confession of O.J. Simpson

He was standing in the middle of the living room, crying.

"My momma's gone! My family . . . my own *niece* . . . she turned on me, said I was guilty! *Kardashian,* he turned out to be a Judas. Who do I got *left*?"

O. J. Simpson was sobbing uncontrollably in the front room of my house. This *was* surreal.

Standing there, I suddenly saw something very clearly about my "guest." Simpson had a fundamental character flaw which in all likelihood had been encouraged in him throughout his adult life. That flaw was his singular inability to perceive himself as he actually was. Whether it was because he was afraid of finding out who that might really be, or because he already knew, the end result was exactly the same: he had developed no instincts for how to survive as a private person. He was the opposite of the boy in the bubble; he could only breathe the air drawn from those around him.

It was now plain to me that without constant reinforcement from his family and friends, and, even more, without uncritical adulation from *his* audience, *his* public, he was completely unable to function as a human being. There was something ineffably sad about this spectacle, despite all of his arrogance and amorality. *Perhaps,* I thought, *the acquittal was actually the worst thing that could have happened to him.* It forced him to walk the halls of his own life, like Banquo's ghost. Little wonder, then, that he used whatever he could to dull the pain.

Watching him, I thought true mercy might well have dictated

that he *had* been given the death penalty. Indeed, what I was witnessing now was a slower, more torturous form of death than any method the state was permitted to use. It was the private execution of a public ego.

CHAPTER ELEVEN

It was hard for me to look at him. Both of us were embarrassed at his having broken down in front of me. Although the crying had stopped, his chest was still heaving and his breathing was coming in spasms.

Reluctantly, I went over to him and lightly touched his shoulder. "O.J., you've got to try and pull it together."

"I know. I *know*. I'm sorry."

He still couldn't look at me. The awkwardness of this scene—both of us standing there while he attempted to regain his composure—quickly became uncomfortable. I said, "Why don't you go sit down on the couch until you feel better."

He gratefully complied.

"Sam," he began, "I fucked up. I know that. I'm not asking you to say it's okay, but I just want you to know I'm sorry. I didn't mean anything by it. It's been really hard for me."

The Confession of O.J. Simpson

I saw what he was trying to do.

"You read that report, right?" He looked at me expectantly.

Instead of sitting with him on the couch, I'd gone over and sat down in the chair opposite him. I was trying to make it very clear I didn't intend to be drawn back into yet another open-ended conversation with him.

"Yes. You know I did. We've already talked about Nicole and Marcus. I still didn't find any of the information you've been promising me all day. Under the circumstances, I really don't think there's anything more I can do for you." This time I would remain firm.

He looked at me and said nothing. Picking up the chopsticks from one of the empty food cartons, he began clicking them together nervously.

"You know, right now I feel like I did that day at Bobby Kardashian's. I was so depressed. They gave me all these pills and shit to make me sleep. . . . But I couldn't sleep and I was in the bedroom when Bobby and Bob Shapiro walked in and Shapiro says, 'O.J. they want you to surrender yourself.' It was like I couldn't hear him. I mean, I heard his voice, but it didn't make no sense to me. I remember they left and I felt like I was underwater. Like that time in Mexico when I got pulled under and I didn't think I could make it back to the beach. I was so tired, man."

His eyes were shut and he was talking slowly, methodically. Like he was in a trance. I didn't interrupt him.

"Bobby came back to pray with me and he got pretty freaked out because he saw I had this gun on my lap. We wound up goin' outside, and A.C. and Bobby tried to get me to put down the gun. Finally, Bobby, he gives up and goes back in the house. He says, 'I can't deal with this anymore. If God wants you, he can have you.'

"So A.C. keeps tryin' to get me to give him the gun and I won't do it. He was freakin' out 'cause I wouldn't even talk to him. He was real happy when I said, 'Let's go for a ride.' It's funny, but I'm sure he thought if we got in the car, I couldn't hurt myself."

At this point he opened his eyes and looked over at me. Maybe he wanted to see if I was paying any attention.

"You know the funny thing, Sam? We didn't *try* to sneak out. We just got in A.C.'s car and left. I figured people had seen us go, but it turns out they didn't know at all. I told A.C. to head over the hill. He got on the freeway and I know he thinks we're goin' to my house. He looked at me real strange when I punched in Nicole's number on the car phone, but he didn't say anything. I don't know why I called. Maybe I just wanted to hear her voice on the machine."

His tone of voice had become distant. For a moment he wasn't talking to me at all. Then he apparently recalled what happened next. He tensed visibly.

"I didn't expect Lou—you know, her dad—to answer the phone. I told him A.C. and me was in the car and he says that he was packing up Nicole's things. I remember saying to him, 'Why are you doing that? You don't know where everything is.' So I told him I was gonna come over and he said okay and hung up.

121

The Confession of O.J. Simpson

"A.C. says to me, 'You really think this is a good idea, Juice? We don't got a lot of time.' At this point I still got the gun on my lap, so I picked it up and I start wavin' it around, right there on the freeway.

"I said, 'A.C., we got as much time as we want.'

"He got real pissed and says, 'Fuck you, O.J. We're in *my* car. The cops are lookin' for you and they're gonna go nuts when they find out you left. You know what this is? This is flight. This is fuckin' flight, and I'm gonna be blamed for it!'

"So I said, 'You won't be blamed for anything. They know you couldn't make me do nothin' I don't wanna do. Look, when we switched clothes at the funeral and the press thought you was me, whose idea was that? Everybody knows you never think of stuff by yourself.'

"A.C. starts screamin' at me to put down the gun and I couldn't stop myself. I just kept fuckin' with him. The madder he was getting, the funnier I thought the whole thing was. So you know what I did?"

If I spoke, it would break his spell. I just shook my head.

"I held the gun right up to A.C.'s head and I said to him, 'You'll just tell them I forced you to drive me, okay? You didn't want to, but I forced you to. I had a gun and you didn't have any choice because you were afraid I'd blow your fucking head off! Okay?'

"He's like, 'Okay, Juice, simmer down. I hear what you're saying. Just, please, put that gun down before somebody sees it.' And I say, 'What are they gonna do? Call the cops?'

"I'm tellin' ya, Sam, we looked at each other—I've got this

122

gun pointed right at his head and we're doing sixty-five on the San Diego freeway—and we both just *lost* it. We both started laughing so hard there was tears runnin' down our cheeks. I had to grab onto the wheel because he almost ran into the car next to us.''

I found myself thinking about Al Cowlings. This guy had grown up with Simpson and he'd obviously gone through hell and back with him that day in the car. That kind of loyalty from a friend, even under those circumstances, was hard not to admire. I said as much to Simpson.

"A.C.? He saved my life so many times, I've lost count. I don't deserve him. That's the truth.'' He stared straight at me, then looked away.

"So we get off the freeway at Sunset and now I'm not feelin' tired anymore. I'm feelin' pretty good. We get to Sunset and Bundy and I tell A.C. to take the shortcut that goes in the back way of Nicole's house. It goes through this alley. As we're headin' down the side street I see these cop cars pulling into the alley right where we're gonna go. I said, 'That fuckin' Lou Brown must've called the cops.' I tell A.C. to just keep driving straight like we wasn't gonna turn. And A.C. says to me, 'Look, man, we really ought to go back to Bobby's.' But I tell him, 'No, just get back on Sunset and head toward the beach.' I knew exactly where we were goin', but I didn't tell A.C. because I didn't want him to turn around.

"He's like, 'I really think we should go back,' but he can tell I got my mind made up, so he just drives where I tell him to. Pretty soon he figures out where we're going. We're in the

Palisades and he says to me, 'Juice, why are we going *here*? Marcus is out of town. We just talked to him last night, remember? He's in the Cayman Islands.'

"I said to him, 'Just keep driving. You'll see.'

"Here's the thing, Sam. A.C. didn't know what happened when I talked to Marcus the night before. I wasn't gonna tell him either. See, Marcus had been calling everybody all week and he was freaking out. He was on some island and he's all upset. The first time I talked to him was right after I got back from Chicago and he kept sayin' he couldn't believe it about Nicole. Then he says, 'I'm so sorry. What can I do? Do you want me to come home?' He wants to get on the next plane and come back for the funeral. At first I just let him talk. I don't let on at all that I know he's been doin' her again. I played it real cool. Like I'm still his big brother, just watchin' out for him. I tell him, 'No, it's okay. You don't have to ruin your trip. Just come back when you're supposed to.'

"Then when I talked to him the day after the funeral, the same time A.C. talked to him, too, I went into the other room and told him that the cops had been asking me all sorts of questions about him and Nicole and I said, 'They're lookin' for any evidence about other guys she knew.' I could just hear him thinking on the other end of the phone, 'Oh my God, now everybody's gonna find out.'

"Of course, he can't tell me that, 'cause he thinks I don't know anything about him and Nicole.

"And then he does exactly what I expected him to do. He

says, 'I feel real bad that I missed the funeral. I'm gonna come home tomorrow. I want to be there for you.' I know what he's *really* thinking is that he's got to make sure there ain't no letters or shit from Nicole still at his house. I made it seem like I was all touched and I said, 'You're a good friend. Call me back and tell me what time you get in.'

"So, he calls me back and says he'll get in around one o'clock. I said, 'Fine. I'll see you tomorrow.' As soon as I hung up the phone I knew what I was gonna do. It would've worked out great, too, except for the fucking cops wanting me to turn myself in. Which is why I made A.C. take me out in the Bronco. I didn't care if the cops had to wait a few hours. I figured they were going to have plenty of time with me anyway. A couple hours more wouldn't make no difference."

As far as I knew, nobody had ever heard this part of the story before. What he was telling me was the Bronco trip was neither an attempted escape nor the spontaneous act of someone looking to commit suicide. He'd planned this trip the night *before,* having no idea he was about to be arrested.

He kept talking.

"When we pulled up in front of Marcus's house, sure enough, his car was out front. I remember A.C. looked at me, like, 'How did you know that?'

"I jumped out of the car and started running up his drive-way. A.C. is tryin' to keep up with me. We get up to his door and I started pounding on it. He opens it, and I thought he was gonna have a heart attack right there. He starts to say, 'What are you doing here?' then he sees I've got the gun in my hand and he just freezes. I stick it right into his chest and I say to him, 'You just had to fuck her again, didn't you?' "

As he described this he was rocking back and forth rapidly. The image of someone in devout prayer sprang into my mind.

"Sam, this guy is a very good football player. He's almost as good as I was. He's taken a lot of hits, but he's never been afraid to go right back up to the line. I'm not kiddin' when I tell you he was really scared. He backs away from the door and says, 'Jesus, O.J., what are you doing?' So I just walked in, still holding the gun on him, and said, 'You are one dumb motherfucker. Who do you think you're messin' with? Don't you think I knew? You've been parkin' your goddamned car in front of her house. Didn't you think I'd figure that out?'

"A.C. starts trying to talk to me. He's all upset. He's like, 'Juice, just leave him alone. What are you doing, man?' And I lost it with him. I said, 'Stay out of this. It's none of your fucking business, and if you say another word I'm gonna blow his motherfucking head off!'

"I remember feelin' like I was watchin' myself do all of this. Like it was somebody else with a gun, not me. I'm standin' there screaming my head off at A.C., who's almost my *brother*, and I'm pointing a gun at Marcus, who everybody says is so like me he might as well *be* my brother. It was a strange feelin', man. Like everything was all slowed down."

He might also have been describing how I was feeling at that moment. Listening to him, it felt like everything was happening to *me* in slow motion. He was telling me he'd threatened to kill Marcus Allen only five days after Nicole and Goldman were killed. Was he finally confirming that he *had* killed them? Had he gone to Marcus's house with the intention of finishing what he'd started on Sunday night?

He'd stopped talking for a moment, like he was waiting for me to say something. All I could manage to get out was, "Then what happened?"

"What do you think happened? Marcus, he starts cryin' like a baby. He's like, 'Don't kill me, man. I didn't mean anything by it. She said she was lonely. She told me you guys were really broken up this time. Don't do this to me, O.J. I'm your friend.' He was beggin' me not to kill him. I wasn't gonna shoot him, but he don't know that. I just wanted him to suffer like I was.

"But it was weird, Sam. As soon as he started crying, it was like somebody flipped off a switch. I didn't hate him anymore. I didn't feel sorry for him. I didn't feel anything. I just looked at him and said, 'You can't have her anymore.' And I turned around and walked out.

"When A.C. and I got back in the car, we didn't talk for a long time. Finally, he said to me, 'Jesus, Juice, I thought you were really gonna lose it back there.' I said, 'I don't want to talk about it anymore.' And we never did. A.C., he never told nobody that we went to see Marcus. Marcus wasn't gonna tell nobody, you can be damn sure. He got right back on a plane and high-tailed it back to that island.

"So now we're back in the Bronco again and I was so tired I felt like I was gonna pass out. A.C. wants to get on the freeway and go back to Bobby's house in the Valley, but I told him I had to see Nicole just one more time first. Instead of going north, I made him turn right and go down to Orange County, to Costa Mesa, where Nicole was. The cops was there, too, so we didn't get to stay very long with her and then we got back on the freeway—and then you know the rest. They started following us back to my house like I was the president and they was my escort. It wasn't no *chase*. I hate it when people call it that. We was just going back to my house. It was no big deal.''

It was hard for me to reconcile O.J.'s casual dismissal of the Bronco ride with the televised images that had burned themselves into the nation's memory.

Finally I asked, ''Whatever happened with you and Marcus?''

''He did come to see me in jail once after that. He wanted me to forgive him. I told him that he shouldn't be talking to me. If he wanted anyone to forgive him, he should be talking to God. That was the last time I ever saw him.''

Chapter twelve

My mind was racing. Before I could pose another question to him, the phone began to ring insistently. For a moment I didn't move, waiting for the machine upstairs to pick it up. After the fourth ring, I remembered I'd left the microcassette tape of Simpson's argument with Nicole in the machine, which meant it wouldn't work.

After six rings, I had no choice but to go out to the kitchen and answer it. "Let me get the phone," I said. "I'll be back in a minute."

Simpson, having finished reliving his wild ride in the Bronco, now appeared completely spent. He didn't seem to have enough energy left to hold himself upright. Indeed, as soon as he'd finished talking, he stretched out on the couch, using one of the cushions for a pillow.

The Confession of O.J. Simpson

I'm going to need a crane just to get him off the couch, I thought.

I got to the kitchen by the tenth ring. Not surprisingly, it was Rachel. She didn't say hello, she just started talking.

"I don't believe you haven't called me. It's eleven-thirty. I wasn't kidding, Sam. I need to have that money by tomorrow. This is no joke."

I said, "I'm sorry I haven't called. I've been really busy. There's a lot going on."

"Laura told me you had O. J. Simpson in *our* house. What was he doing there?"

"He's come to see me on a legal matter. I'm talking to him about whether or not I can help him."

"What do you mean? He's still there? My God, Sam! You've had him there all day?"

"We're just about done. Can I call you in the morning?"

"No, we've got to settle this tonight. Are you going to give me the money or not? I need to know now."

"Rachel, I've got to finish preparing my brief for the Belli hearing. You know that's all I've had time to do. A few of my clients do owe me money, but I haven't even had the time to call them."

"That's just like you. Money never means anything to you. So what you're telling me is you don't have it, is that right?"

I was in no mood to argue with her. So I decided to lie.

"I'll have it. I'll get it for you tomorrow. Just wait till the morning and I'll make some calls."

Even over the phone her sigh was audible. After a moment she said, "What choice do I have?"

She still wasn't done with me, though.

"Sam, I won't have Simpson being around Laura. He's a monster. He ought to be in jail, and I don't want him around my daughter."

On this point we had no argument. I said, "Believe me, I agree with you. I didn't plan on him being here to begin with, and I certainly didn't expect Laura to show up at the same time. She won't ever see him again, I promise."

He was sitting alone in my living room. I had to get off the phone.

"Rachel, I've really got to go. I'll get you the money to-morrow."

"You'd better. I meant what I said in my message."

"What are you talking about?" I asked, feigning ignorance.

"Don't you listen to your machine? I don't know why you even have one. What I said was if you don't get me those checks by tomorrow, then I'm taking you to court. That's a promise."

"All right, Rachel. Good-bye."

The phone clicked in my ear. She hadn't exactly hung up on me, but she hadn't said good-bye either.

I went back into the living room. Simpson was curled up on the couch, his legs drawn up to his chest. He was sound asleep. The sleep of the innocent, I thought bitterly. Leaving me awake to wrestle with a choice I didn't know if I could make.

I shut off the television and turned off all the downstairs

lights. Then I locked the front door and walked wearily upstairs. I had to go to bed.

My office lamp was still on. As I walked over to the desk to turn it off, I suddenly thought of something Rachel had said on the phone. *Don't you listen to your machine? I don't know why you even have one.*

Something clicked, and I remembered the plastic pouch containing the microcassettes. I still hadn't gone through them. It was almost midnight. I'd gone past the point of exhaustion hours ago, but I knew I wouldn't be able to sleep now until I'd at least listened to those tapes.

It's funny, I thought to myself, *Simpson is the one who used cocaine and he's sound asleep right now. Yet as tired as I am, I can't make myself go to sleep.*

I took the cassettes out of the pouch and stacked them on top of the answering machine. There were eight of them. I sat on the edge of the desk and put my reading glasses on so that I could read the tiny print on each tape. They were all individually dated and I strained to make out what was written on each of them. One was from May. Two were from April. Another was from February and there were three from December. I knew none of these could have any significance to Simpson's hypothetical "confession."

I hit pay dirt with the eighth tape. It was dated June 11, the day before the murders. Both sides of the tape had been used, which meant it might contain as much as two hours of recording. Side one had *A.M.* printed on it. I flipped it over. The other side was marked *P.M.* I took the tape I'd listened to earlier out of the answering machine and put this one in, starting with the A.M. side face-up. I pressed *message.*

The first thing I heard was a lot of street traffic and background noise. This lasted for almost a minute until a female voice said, *"O.J., what are you doing here?"* It was Nicole.

Simpson: I just got back into town.

Nicole: You can't just show up like this. How did you know I was here?

Simpson: I saw the Ferrari on the street and then I saw you sitting out here by yourself.

Nicole: What are you doing now? Cruising around the neighborhood looking for my car?

Simpson: First of all, it's my car. I paid for it. And second, it's a little hard to miss with that license plate you got on it. You know, I think it looks real bad, you driving the kids around in a car that says "late for a date."

Nicole: You know what, O.J.? I don't care what you think. Why don't you just go?

Simpson: Why? Are you expecting someone?

Nicole: As a matter of fact, I'm here with someone. He's just gone inside to get our coffee. He'll be right back.

It sounded like they were at some outdoor café. Simpson had clearly taken her by surprise by showing up. He also must have had a tape recorder concealed on him somewhere. I thought back to his explanation for taping Laura earlier. *You wanna know*

133

The Confession of O. J. Simpson

why I keep a tape recorder in my pocket all the time now? Remember, I'm O. J. Simpson. I'm guilty until proven innocent.

But the tape I was listening to now had been made on June 11, *before* he was ever accused of anything. The existence of all these microcassettes meant that he'd been recording his private conversations for a long time prior to the murders. Years earlier, before Simpson and Nicole were even married, he'd somehow found a way to tape the telephone conversation they'd had about the incident with Frank Sinatra in Las Vegas. It now appeared he was utilizing much more sophisticated technology to record everything and everybody in his life.

Simpson: Which one is he?

Nicole: The one with the dark hair, by the cash register.

Simpson: The kid?

Nicole: He's not a kid and he has a name. It's Ron.

Simpson: Ron. Why don't you tell Ron you need to talk to me and you'll see him later?

Simpson elongated the name Ron when he said it. I could hear the sarcasm in his voice.

Nicole: Because I don't want to talk to you. I'm not happy with you right now.

Simpson: What did I do?

Nicole: I don't want to talk about it here. Can you just please leave?

A Work of Fiction

Simpson: I've got a right to be here. It's a public street. And you're my wife.

Nicole: You're not . . . look, he's coming. Can you just go?

Simpson lowered his voice to a whisper and I could barely hear him.

Simpson: Introduce me.

There was the sound of metal scraping. A chair being pulled out? Then another voice spoke. A male voice. He said, *"Hi."*

Nicole: Ron, this is my . . . this is O.J. O.J., this is Ron Goldman.

Goldman: Good to meet you.

Simpson: She's still my wife, you know.

Nicole: O.J., for God sakes, I'm not your wife. You've got to stop doing this.

Goldman: I don't understand. I thought . . .

Nicole: We *are* divorced, Ron. He just gets a little confused about it sometimes.

Simpson: Look, I need to talk to you about the kids.

Nicole: What about them?

Simpson: When are you bringing them over today?

Nicole: Noon. Like every Saturday. You know that, O.J.

Simpson: Well, if I'm not there, just have Arnelle watch them.

135

The Confession of O. J. Simpson

Nicole: If you're not going to be there, why am I bringing them over at all?

Simpson: Just bring them. I'll be back later on. Did you get my ticket for the recital?

Nicole: I already told you I did. Can't we talk about this later?

Simpson: Yeah. Fine. I'll see you at the house.

Nicole: Good-bye, O.J.

Goldman: Nice to meet you.

Simpson: Yeah.

The recorder had obviously been switched off and then switched back on again. It sounded like Ron Goldman was in the middle of a sentence when it started to record again.

Goldman: . . . waiting for me?

Simpson: Yeah, I wanted to tell you I was sorry for what happened back there at the Starbucks. I just needed to talk to Nicole for a minute.

Goldman: How did you know where I live?

Simpson: I was driving and I seen you walking from here before.

Goldman: I'm sorry. I still don't understand. We only just met a few minutes ago. How did you notice me walking before you even met me?

Simpson: I know who you are.

Goldman: What do you mean?

A Work of Fiction

Simpson: I know you're one of Nic's friends. I've seen you driving the car.

Goldman: I've driven it a few times. She told me I could use it when I didn't have my car.

Simpson: You gotta be real careful when you drive that car. Ferraris are real expensive to keep up. I should know. I get all the bills.

Goldman: I'm very careful.

Simpson: I don't mean to hassle you. You seem like a nice guy. I just wanted to tell you that Nicole and I are still trying to work things out.

Goldman: That's not what she told me.

Simpson: She don't know what she's sayin' most of the time. One day she tells me one thing, the next day it's something completely different. You know how women are.

Goldman: I don't understand why you're telling me all this.

Simpson: Because she likes you and I don't want you to get the wrong idea and maybe get hurt.

Goldman: Thank you. I can take care of myself.

Simpson: I'm sure you can. I'm just sayin' that she's a little confused right now. Listen, man, Nicole and me have been together for seventeen years. I know this girl. She goes through head trips and puts everyone else through 'em at the same time. Like, it was just her birthday and she was real sick, so who does she call? She calls me. And I drop everything to go over and take care of her. Give her food, watch the kids. She's in bed all day and I did everything. I gave her this expensive brace-let. It was antique. I paid more than twenty thou-

137

sand dollars for it. And you know what she did? As soon as she got better, she gives it back to me and says, "I don't want anything from you." You see what I'm talkin' about? She totally changes her mind all the time. You never know which end is up with her.

Goldman: What does any of this have to do with me?

Simpson: Well, right now you seem to be her flavor of the week, and I thought you should know what you're gettin' yourself into.

Goldman: Look, Mr. Simpson—O.J.—I appreciate your concern. What I don't appreciate is you following me. And I know Nicole doesn't either.

Simpson: I told you I wasn't following you. I just happened to see where you live. Nicole gets all paranoid. She always thinks people are following her.

Goldman: Look, it's none of my business, but she told me that she's seen you following her.

Simpson: You're right. It ain't none of your business. But what happens with my family is my business. Don't forget that.

Goldman: You're not threatening me, are you?

Simpson: Hey, no, man. I'm just givin' you some friendly advice, that's all.

Goldman: Then thanks for the advice. I've gotta go inside. I'm gonna be late.

Simpson: Yeah, you go. I don't mean to hold you up or nothing. I'm sure you've got things to do. I'll see you around.

Goldman: Yeah. See ya.

A Work of Fiction

I could hear the sound of someone walking, probably Simpson, and then apparently the recorder had been turned off again. The tape continued to run in my answering machine for a few minutes, although there wasn't anything else on it. When I was sure of this, I hit *stop* and took the tape out.

I was certain that Simpson's conversation with Goldman had never been reported anywhere. It would have been a bombshell at the criminal trial. Although he was careful not to threaten Goldman explicitly, Simpson made it clear that Goldman should watch himself around Nicole.

What impressed me about Ron Goldman, even on the tape, was his willingness to stand up to Simpson. It would have been understandable for him to be intimidated by such an imposing figure. Yet he stood his ground. Not for a moment did he give in to Simpson's bullying.

What was it Goldman had said on the tape? *I can take care of myself.* By all accounts he did, in fact, fight heroically to take care of himself—and Nicole—the very next night.

I'd just heard a recording of the opening round of that fight.

CHAPTER THIRTEEN

There was no way to fast-forward the tape on my answering machine, but it did have a rewind button. I put the tape back in the machine, this time with the P.M. side facing up, and I rewound it to the beginning.

The first sound I heard seemed to be of metal clanging. A gate closing? Then the sound of footsteps on pavement and a light rapping that could only have been someone knocking on a door. Then voices.

Simpson: Thanks for letting me come over. I'm sorry I wasn't home when you dropped off the kids to-day.

Nicole: It's okay. Why are you all dressed up?

The Confession of O. J. Simpson

Her voice sounded very different than it had that morning. She seemed tired but not angry. Her tone was neutral, even a bit friendly.

Simpson: I was at this thing for the prime minister of Israel's wife. Lots of heavy hitters. Twenty-five-thousand-dollar tickets. It was for some Jewish charity.

Nicole: That tux still looks good on you. I bought that for you in New York.

Simpson: I remember.

Nicole: You wanna come in?

Simpson: Sure. Thanks. Hi, Kato. Good boy.

The sound of a door closing. There were more footsteps now, but they sounded different, hollow. Hardwood floors? I also heard what had to be the sound of a dog, its nails clicking on the floor in the frenzy of enthusiasm that comes from seeing someone it recognized.

Nicole: Talk quietly. I just got Sydney to go back to sleep a few minutes ago.

Simpson: Why was she up so late?

Nicole: She's very excited about tomorrow. Today was the dress rehearsal. She looks so adorable in her outfit. Wait till you see her.

Simpson: You know, Paula really wanted to go tomorrow, but I told her it was only for family. She didn't like that too much.

A Work of Fiction

Nicole: You can bring her, if you want. I don't know if I can get another ticket, though.

Simpson: It's okay. I don't really need to. She wants to go to everything. Like I took her to this thing tonight and she was talkin' to everybody like she was the queen bee.

Nicole: Well, you're lucky she enjoys all those things. You know I don't.

Simpson: I know. But you're a million times better at it than she is. She works way too hard at it. You just hang back and everybody notices you. That's why you're so good at it. It also don't hurt that you're the most beautiful woman in the room.

Nicole: What happened to Paula tonight?

Simpson: I took her home early. I told her I was tired. What I really was, was tired of her.

Nicole: You know Faye is in rehab again.

Simpson: About time, too. She was losin' it.

Nicole: She's been a good friend to me. I want her to get better.

Simpson: Do we have to talk about her?

Nicole: You know, I shouldn't even be talking to you at all after what you did.

Simpson: What did I do?

Nicole: You know exactly what you did. You sent me that letter and now we have to move. I just don't believe you could do that. Even if you wanted to hurt me, do you know how hard this is gonna be for the kids? This will be their third move in three years. That's not fair, O.J.

143

The Confession of O. J. Simpson

Simpson: What are talkin' about, Nic? I don't want you to move.

Nicole: Don't pretend you don't know what this is about. That letter said you'd report me to the IRS if I continue to use Rockingham as my legal residence. Now I have to rent this place out or I'll get hit with a big tax bill that I can't afford to pay. It doesn't matter whether you admit it or not. I don't care anymore. You got your way. We're moving to Malibu next month.

Simpson: Nic, you gotta believe me. I didn't mean for you to have to move. Do you think I'd do that to the kids? No way. Skip made me write that letter for legal reasons. He said I had to protect myself in case the IRS started looking at me. I don't want you to go to Malibu. That's too far.

Nicole: You should have thought of that sooner.

Simpson: Look, I'll call Skip on Monday and we'll get this all worked out. I'll do whatever it takes. If you still need to move, then I'll help you find a place closer. I'll even pay for the move.

Nicole: O.J., it's not about the money. You always try to buy your way out of everything. That letter hurt me. You can't do things like that to people.

Simpson: I'm sorry, sweets. You're right. I didn't think. I'm really sorry. You gotta let me fix it.

Nicole: O.J., I already put a deposit down.

Simpson: That don't matter. If they won't give it back, I'll give it back to you. Like you said, it's only money.

Nicole: Did you just hear something?

A Work of Fiction

Simpson: Maybe. Is the TV on?

Nicole: Yeah, I left it on in my bedroom, but I thought I
           heard one of the kids. I'm gonna go up and check.

Simpson: Can I come with you?

Nicole: Okay, but please be very quiet. Sydney has a big
           day tomorrow.

Simpson: I will. I will.

A minute passed with neither of them speaking. Then, I
heard Nicole's voice again, whispering.

Nicole: They're asleep. It must have been the television.

He responded in what was probably intended to be a whisper. There was little difference from his regular voice. As loud
as he was, it was amazing that the kids didn't wake up.

Simpson: She's an angel. Just like her mother.

I could hear a door quietly close and then the sound of a
television, faint at first, growing steadily louder, probably because they were walking toward it. Finally, the sound of another
door clicking shut. Then they started talking again in their normal voices.

Simpson: I really want to get out of this tux. I've got some
           sweats here, don't I?

Nicole: Yes, they're down there in that bottom drawer.

The Confession of O. J. Simpson

At this point their voices on the tape became muffled, as if something was placed over the microphone. I guessed that Simpson had left the tape recorder running in the jacket of his tuxedo, maybe in the breast pocket. If he was changing into a sweatsuit, he'd probably lay the jacket and pants over a chair so he could easily grab them when he left. *If* he left.

Simpson: This fat guy's so funny. I love this guy. Turn it up.

Nicole: Not too much louder. They can sometimes hear it even with the door closed.

I could hear the television more distinctly now. Someone was shouting something about *livin' in a van, down by the river.* That was followed by a little laughter. This was all the tape picked up for at least three or four minutes until the sound of the television was abruptly cut off. Now I could hear them talking again.

Simpson: This is nice.

Nicole: Uh-huh.

Simpson: Just a little?

Nicole: It's very late. I have to be up early tomorrow.

Simpson: I don't want to stay. I'm teeing off at six. Come on, Nic. Just for a little while.

They stopped talking, and although I could still hear some occasional sounds, they were so faint that I wasn't able to make

146

out anything specific. I had a pretty good idea of what was happening, though.

Suddenly the television came back on. Had they started watching it again or had one of them hit the remote control by accident? The voice from the television was familiar. Wasn't that Charlton Heston? What was he doing on a comedy show? I thought for a moment about when this was happening. The murders had taken place on a Sunday, I remembered that. So this was very late Saturday night. Sure, that made sense. They were watching *Saturday Night Live*. Charlton Heston was probably hosting the show.

I kept listening, waiting for either Simpson or Nicole to start speaking again, but for a good five minutes all I heard was Heston doing a takeoff on *Planet of the Apes*. Then the television's volume got much softer and I could hear them talking in low, urgent tones.

Nicole: You're tired. Why don't you just go home and get some sleep?

Simpson: Just play with it a little more.

Nicole: O.J. . . .

Simpson: Dammit, Nicole, just play with it.

Nicole: I'm really tired, O.J. We both are. Maybe you can come over tomorrow night after the recital.

Simpson: Goddammit, this pisses me off. Why did you have to get me so upset before?

Nicole: Oh, please. You're not trying to blame this on me, are you?

147

The Confession of O.J. Simpson

They were talking over each other now; it was becoming difficult to clearly understand what they were saying.

Simpson: Come on. It's starting. . . .

Nicole: Stop doing this to yourself, you're—

Simpson: Just suck on . . .

Nicole: . . . too tired . . .

Simpson: . . . little, it will . . .

Nicole: It's okay. . . .

Simpson: . . . not okay . . . you always . . .

Nicole: I didn't. . . .

Simpson: . . . get me all stressed out . . .

Nicole's voice became more audible. Had she moved closer to the recorder? And away from him?

Nicole: This wasn't my idea to begin with.

Simpson: Yeah. I know all about your ideas. That little white boy, he's your idea, ain't he? You probably fucked him all day and that's why you don't care what happens now.

Nicole: Here we go again. You really need to leave, O.J. I'm too tired to go through all this shit with you tonight.

Simpson: How come you're in such a big hurry to get rid of me? You got him comin' over?

Nicole: O.J., that's enough. He's just a friend. That's all. You're trying to make something out of nothing.

A Work of Fiction

Simpson: Yeah? I'm makin' somethin' out of nothing? I'll tell you what's nothing. Nothing is what you said you were doing with Marcus. Nothing is what's supposed to be happening when I'm out of town, but Marcus has got his car parked in front of your house. Your nothing is just a bunch of bullshit.

Nicole: Keep your voice down. I swear I'll kill you if you wake them up again.

He ignored her and continued to shout.

Simpson: Don't tell me what to do. That's your problem. You're always trying to tell me what to do.

Nicole: I can't believe it. You really were having me followed. What the fuck is wrong with you? Why can't you just leave me alone?

She was crying now.

Simpson: I'm gonna leave you alone. When I'm done with you, everyone'll leave you alone. I'm gonna tell them all what a slut you are, and then you're really gonna know what it feels like to be alone. Your friend, Faye, is gonna be the only one you got left. You two are perfect for each other. That's right, bitch. You run. Just get the fuck out of my sight. You're too ugly for me to look at anyway. I'm outta here.

The tape kept going. Somebody on *Saturday Night Live* was repeating the phrase *"buh bye."* I heard the rustling of clothes and then the hollow footsteps again, followed by the sound of shoes on pavement. The sharp, metallic sound of the gate was much louder this time than before.

Abruptly, the tape ended.

I stared at the machine. Then I got up from my desk, so drained I felt physically sick. I wasn't sure that I would make it to my bedroom. I did, barely. The last thing I remember thinking was, *I need to take off my shoes.*

CHAPTER FOURTEEN

The next morning Simpson and I went to Starbucks for coffee. It was a different Starbucks than any I'd ever seen before. For one thing, it was situated on the very top of a hotel tower. And it was also revolving slowly, providing a three-hundred-and-sixty-degree view of the city. I commented on the great view of the water, although I wasn't sure which direction I was facing in. Simpson didn't look up from the menu, but said, "Don't get too close to the window or you'll get sick."

It was a beautiful day, so we went outside on the deck. My daughter, Laura, who was waitressing that day, came over and brought us our fruit drinks in two large glasses. I noticed his had a little parasol and mine didn't. I started to say something, but Simpson began yelling: "This is bullshit. I didn't order this. You know what I want. I always get the same thing here." Laura called her manager over, a large black man in a business suit.

The Confession of O.J. Simpson

His nameplate read A.C. He ignored Simpson and said to me, "I'm sorry, sir, but you'll have to leave." I protested and said, "What did I do?" but he wasn't listening. I looked over at Simpson for support and he was pointing a gun at me. He said, "If I'm goin' down, you're goin' down with me." Then he, Laura, and A.C. all doubled over in laughter. I was getting really angry at this point, but they didn't seem to care or even notice.

A large white dog came up and started sniffing at Simpson, who reached down to pet him. I said to Laura, "I didn't know you allowed dogs in here." She said, "We don't." Then the dog started foaming at the mouth and I said to Laura, "Don't touch him, he has rabies."

It was such a sunny day that I went to the beach. When I started walking on the sand, I noticed my shoes were getting sand in them, so I sat down on the towel next to Nicole and Rachel, who were sunbathing. They were both topless and I thought, *Rachel needs to be careful because she burns easily.* "Have you seen, O.J.?" I asked them. They said they hadn't, but that he was fine and could take care of himself. I said, "He can't swim," and then I saw him out in the water, yelling and thrashing about. I ran down to the water and waded in up to my chest. I got close enough to see he was in trouble, but a wave broke over both of us before I could reach him. I didn't get wet, but he went under and I grabbed him and started pulling him to shore. He was very heavy and I remember thinking he could pull us both under. I said, "You've got to help me or this won't work," and that got him upset. He started flailing about, trying to pull himself loose from me. He punched me on the shoulder and I said, "You can't do that to people."

Simpson was shaking me awake. "Sam? Hey Sam, c'mon, you gotta get up. It's six-thirty. We have to go."

Usually it took me very little time to wake up. I had the ability—I've had it my whole life—to come right out of a deep sleep and immediately begin thinking clearly and speaking in full sentences.

Not this morning. The inside of my head was as shrouded in fog as the city often was at this hour. I didn't yet know if there was fog outside on this particular morning, since my eyes weren't open wide enough to see out the window.

"It's so early," I mumbled.

"Not for me, man. I've usually finished three holes of golf by now."

Good for you, I thought. *I'm usually still asleep now.* My growing irritation at being woken up so early was also what prevented me from getting back to sleep. It occurred to me that the only thing worse than dealing with Simpson was having to do so at this ungodly hour. I still wasn't sure how I wanted to proceed with him, if at all. But I couldn't imagine any circumstances under which I'd be willing to leave the house in his company.

"What do you mean, we have to go?" It was more a growl than a question.

"There's someplace I wanna take you."

"O.J., I *can't.* I've already lost an entire day with you. I just don't have any more time to spend on this now."

The Confession of O. J. Simpson

As I continued talking, my mind finally started to clear from its half-wakened state. I now remembered listening to the June 11 tape and simultaneously realized this *wasn't* something I'd just dreamed.

I blurted it out. "That tape marked June eleven. It sounds like it was made . . . like it was done on the night of the murders."

"You heard that, huh?"

"Yes."

"No, it was from the day before. We had a big fight that night. I left."

"Nobody ever found this out? How is that possible?"

"Easy. I never told nobody. Nobody but me and Nicole knew I was even there. Paula didn't know. And I still got up and played eighteen holes the next morning. Shot a lousy round, though."

That he had golfed poorly on the morning of his ex-wife's murder hardly seemed any cause for sympathy. I sat up in bed and looked at him. He was bare-chested (no doubt he'd taken off the Clinton T-shirt as soon as he woke up) and leaning against the chest of drawers opposite my bed. His polo shirt was draped over his arm.

"I really do have to get back to work today, O.J."

Before answering me, he pulled the polo shirt on over his head. He'd clearly scrubbed it thoroughly this morning, because, as far as I could tell, there wasn't a trace of blood remaining on it. With his own shirt back on, he shifted into take-charge mode, hoping that the sheer momentum of his words would carry me along with him one more time.

"Sam. I never asked you to do this for free, did I? You know that's true. Now that you seen what I brought you, you gotta know how much that's worth. And I still need you to write up what I gotta say to Goldman. That's what we gotta do today. I'll make you a deal. Just come with me for a little while now, and if you tell me after that that you don't want no part of the rest of it—Goldman and that part—then I'll pay you for your time and we're still friends, okay?"

"O.J., I—"

"Whaddya charge an hour? Two-fifty?"

It was one seventy-five, but I didn't correct him. He wasn't listening to me anyway.

"How many hours is that? Let's see. . . . I got here before noon and we was up to almost midnight. That's . . . what is that?"

"Twelve hours," I said.

"Twelve hours plus another couple of hours now, that's thirteen . . . that's fourteen hours. So at two-fifty an hour, how much do I owe you now?"

I multiplied silently.

"Thirty-five hundred dollars."

"Only thirty-five hundred? That's nowhere near enough. You're worth a lot more than that. If you come with me this morning, right now, we'll call it five thousand for everything."

"O.J., this isn't about—"

The Confession of O. J. Simpson

"Ten thousand dollars, Sam. That's as high as I'll go, but I'll write you a check right now, before we leave."

A check. I'd promised Rachel that I'd have her check and Laura's check this morning. Unfortunately, that hadn't been a dream either. What he'd just offered me would cover both of those checks and this month's mortgage payment, which was already late.

It was only a couple of hours. . . .

"Where is it you want to go?"

He was smiling that smile again. The one that said: *I love it when I get what I want.*

"I'll tell you when we're in the car. Do you mind driving? I don't have much gas and I need what I got to get back to my mom's place later."

I actually preferred it. By driving, I might be able to exercise some control over how long this would take.

"No, that's fine. Just give me a minute to clean up and change my clothes."

When I got downstairs, he was sitting in the overstuffed chair, reading the newspaper. I had short, vivid image of my neighbors seeing him retrieve the paper from the front walk, but I put it quickly out of my mind. There was nothing I could do about it, anyway.

"So, where are we going?" I asked him again when we got in the car.

"Isn't it a beautiful morning, man? God, I love San Francisco."

A Work of Fiction

He was oddly serene. After listening to his disembodied voice on the tapes the night before, it now felt unreal to hear him speaking aloud again.

"O.J., I can't just drive. Tell me where we're going."

"Keep going, man. We're fine. I'll tell you where to go. It's not far."

It occurred to me this was precisely how Cowlings must have felt.

We made a right on Dolores Street and stayed on it until it turned into San Jose Avenue. After a few blocks it became the 280 Freeway heading south, and we continued on that. In less than five miles, we were out of the city of San Francisco proper.

We passed through Daly City, and now we were entering the tiny town of Colma. It was here that Simpson directed me to get off the highway.

"Turn left and head up that hill."

It dawned on me where we were going. Given the small geographic size of the city of San Francisco, open tracts of land were scarce and at a premium. By necessity, this meant no cemeteries were located within the actual city limits. Less expensive areas like Colma had inevitably become the burial ground for people making their final departure from the Bay Area. With Simpson's mother having passed away only recently, I was certain he was going to visit her one last time before returning to Los Angeles.

We pulled up to the wrought-iron gates of the cemetery, only to discover they were locked. A sign on one of the brick pillars adjacent to the gate noted that visiting hours were between eight A.M. and six P.M. Given it was still only seven-thirty, it seemed he was out of luck.

He didn't see it that way. He jumped out of the car, leaving the passenger door open, and before I could even ask "What are you doing?" he was up and over the fence. He landed like a perfect gymnast, his arms extended over his head with no stutter step required to break the fall. When he turned around to face me, he was smiling that half-smile again. It was an invitation to join him.

I reached over and pulled the passenger door shut, then put the car in reverse, parking by the sidewalk that ran along the fence in front of the grounds. I got out and walked over to where I could speak to him through the gate.

"You don't really expect me to do that, too?" I asked.

"C'mon, Sam. It's easy. You don't have to do it like I did. Just climb up slowly and I'll help you down on this side. My mom's here, I want you to come see her with me, okay?"

The gate was about seven feet high. Its vertical metal bars were each sharply pointed at the apex, making it impossible to straddle the gate at the top. I took all this in, then slowly began my ascent.

"That's it, Sam. You can do it. No problem."

I felt like I was back in junior high school trying to climb the rope in gym class. Simpson had taken the part of the coach, and he was playing it with enthusiasm.

"Okay, now just put your hands on the crossbar between the arrows"—the metal points did resemble outsize arrowheads—"and then swing your legs, one at a time, over to this side."

I did as he instructed, and as soon as my second leg was completely over the top, I felt his hands grabbing me firmly at the waist.

"Just let go now," he ordered.

Instead of letting me fall, he held on to me, lowering me gently to the ground.

"Thanks," I said.

"No problem. It's up here."

We walked up a slight incline along the gravel path bisecting the cemetery. After about two minutes, he pointed to a particular spot on the side of the hill and we began navigating our own way over the grass, weaving in and out between the marble head-stones and simple white crosses that marked the graves.

When we approached the still-fresh patch of earth that was his mother's final resting place, I lagged behind him for a few steps and then stopped entirely, allowing him to arrive at the spot by himself.

After only a moment at the grave, he looked around and saw I wasn't behind him.

"It's okay, Sam. Come on over. I'd like you to see her."

I walked over to where he was standing. Her grave was one of those that didn't have a headstone. There were, however, fresh flowers in front of the white cross, indicating someone had been here recently.

"My sisters," said Simpson, noticing me looking at the flowers. "They took care of everything . . . the funeral, every-

159

thing. I tell 'em all the time they're too good for this world. They really are. Just like my momma was.''

He was talking to me, but his eyes were somewhere else.

''My mom was incredible, man. You know I had rickets when I was a little kid? I did. She couldn't afford no braces for me—that was about the time my dad left—so she made 'em herself out of two shoes and an iron bar. I wouldn't even be *walking* today if she hadn't done that for me. Forget about football. I love her so much, man. She is the best. Always will be.''

I felt I should say something.

''You're lucky to have had her for so long.''

''That's the truth. It wasn't easy for her these last years, but she stayed strong so I would too, you know? It don't matter what anyone says about me, I'm her boy and no one messes with me around her. Not Connie Chung, not nobody. She told 'em all where to get off.''

He kept referring to her as though she were still alive. And to him, she was.

''I wish I'd brought her flowers. She loves those big yellow ones.''

I thought of something and walked several feet away from where we were standing. Looking around on the ground near the shrubbery, I found two small stones. I walked back to Simpson and gave him one. The other I placed on top of the crosspiece of his mother's marker.

''What's that for?'' He was puzzled.

''It's a Jewish tradition. We commemorate the grave of a

loved one by leaving a small stone when we come to visit. It signifies that we honor their memory.''

''That's real nice. I like that a lot.'' He put his stone next to mine, then lowering himself on one knee, he made an invisible cross on his chest.

''Sam, give me a hand, will ya? My knee locks and it's hard for me to get up.''

I reached out to him and he took hold of my arm. Grimacing, he slowly straightened himself up to his full height. One moment he was leaping over a fence, the next he had trouble standing without help. In every way, he was a study in contrasts.

We turned away from his mother's grave and began walking down the hill. Then suddenly he stopped, like he'd remembered something. He scanned the ground back and forth, as if he were looking for a golf ball lost in the rough. Reaching down, he picked up a small rock and walked quickly back up the hill with it.

Curious, I followed him.

Instead of going to his mother's spot, he went a few feet away to a simple gray headstone. I got close enough to read the name: JIMMIE LEE SIMPSON 1919–1985. He put the rock on top of the headstone and, without a word, turned around and walked back down the hill.

Even though it was not quite eight o'clock, I was relieved to see that the main gate was now open, thus precluding my repeat performance as Spider-Man.

The guard at the main entrance looked sharply at us for a

moment, obviously angry that we were inside without his knowledge. Then, as if a light went on, he recognized Simpson. His demeanor changed in an instant.

"Morning, Mr. Simpson. Glad to see you, sir. Your sisters were here yesterday."

Simpson smiled and waved, not breaking stride. I thought of Tiger Woods.

"Thanks, Billy. I'll be back in a couple weeks. Got to make a plane." He said this all over his shoulder, having already reached the car. I was right behind him.

"Good luck to you, Mr. Simpson. God bless you."

We heard Billy's words through the open car window as we were pulling away.

"So, I guess I'll take you back to your car," I said as we got back on the highway.

"No, there's one more stop we have to make."

Sensing I was about to protest, he spoke first.

"I promised you a confession, Sam. Now that's what I'm gonna give you."

CHAPTER FIFTEEN

We arrived at the Potrero Hill Recreation Center in San Francisco about 8:20 A.M. It didn't open until nine o'clock, but
this time, thankfully, there was no high fence to climb. The small
gate was easily navigated and we were able to get inside the
courtyard with no difficulty.

I could immediately see why he'd come here.

The recreation center itself was a large stucco building that
resembled a high-school gym or auditorium. High on the wall
above the main doors to the building was a larger-than-life-size
mural depicting various athletic pursuits. A boy was swinging a
baseball bat. There was a young girl doing gymnastics. Two boys
were shooting hoops. The fourth and final image was of a man
running with a football tucked under his arm. He wore a helmet
and a dark blue-and-white uniform with the number 32 embla-
zoned on his chest. Simpson's number.

The Confession of O. J. Simpson

He was standing underneath it, facing me. What immediately came to my mind was an image from the movie *Patton,* where George C. Scott struts onto the screen in front of a giant American flag. At first it dwarfs him, then he seems to grow larger and larger as the flag recedes into the background.

"See that guy up there, Sam? That's The Juice. He still means a lot to people around here. This is my old neighborhood. It's where I grew up. I lived right down that hill, in those projects. I played baseball on that field right over there. I wanted to be a catcher. You know I met Willie Mays when I was just a kid? It's true."

The Simpson standing in front of me seemed to grow taller and more confident with every word.

"I remember when they finished that painting up there, they had this big ceremony. Everybody from around here, my family, everybody came. Even some of the Superiors, the guys I used to run with back in school. They was all puffed up, talkin' about how they used to hang with The Juice and how impressed all their friends was when they told 'em they knew me.

"I let every one of 'em have his picture taken with me that day. And you know, while we were standing there they'd sorta be tellin' me their life story. One guy, Frank, he was a bus driver. Another guy, Mickey, he was a security guard. A couple of them, they done some time. But you know, every single one of them said, wherever they go, if they tell people they know The Juice, it was like doors would open up for 'em. It was like I was the biggest thing they had going for them in their lives, you see

164

what I'm sayin'? Some of these guys, I ain't seen 'em for fifteen or twenty years, and they're probably still making it seem like I'm their best friend. You know what? I don't mind it. They can pretend to be good friends with me if it makes 'em feel important. You gotta give something back to people, Sam. It's the only way you ever get to heaven.''

The center was located in a residential neighborhood, and people were starting to leave for work. Simpson picked up on my discomfiture and said, ''Let's go 'round back. No one can see us from there.''

As we were walking on the dirt path that ran alongside the building, he reached into his pocket and handed me the micro-cassette recorder.

''You know how to use one of these?'' he asked.

''I think so,'' I replied, looking down at the tiny device in my palm.

''Good. You're gonna need it.''

In back of the recreation center was a children's play area with swings, a jungle gym, and a seesaw. Beyond it to the north was a striking view of downtown San Francisco. I thought how hard it must be for someone growing up here; being able to see San Francisco so clearly, yet never really being able to touch it. It was easy to see why, after Simpson literally ran his way out of here, he chose never to move back.

He sat down in one of the children's swings, the frame groaning under his two hundred pounds. His feet were planted in the sand and he was gripping the chains of the swing with both hands. I stood only about a foot away, holding the small tape recorder in front of me like a reporter, waiting for him to start speaking.

He looked at me. "Ready?"

I pressed the record button and the red light came on. "Ready," I said.

Simpson took a deep breath and began speaking slowly. He was more deliberate in his choice of words than he'd ever been with me before.

"I'm going to tell you how it could have gone down. This is the story we're giving to Goldman and he can believe it if he wants to. Understand?"

I nodded. For some reason I didn't want my voice to be heard on this tape.

"The first thing you got to remember is that The Juice wouldn't be sitting around his house all depressed and unhappy, like they tried to make out in court. The Juice has too much goin' on in his life for that. Anybody who knows him will tell you that. If he had a trip to Chicago that night, he'd be packing, talking on the phone, hitting golf balls, he'd do all of those things. Where people mess up is when they say he was either packing *or* sleeping *or* swinging a club . . . he was doin' all of that. And more stuff, too. He'd be hungry and would want to get some quick food. Those red-eye flights don't serve too much. His office would have sent him traveling money from the bank and there'd only be hundreds in the envelope. Of course he'd ask Kato for something smaller if he was only going to Mc-Donald's. And you gotta figure, Kato being Kato, he *would*

166

invite himself along. If you're The Juice, you're used to this kinda shit happening to you all the time, so you don't make a big deal out of it. Listen, if The Juice had been planning to do something later, believe me, he wouldn't be using Kato for an alibi. When God was passing out brains, Kato was standing behind the door, you know what I'm sayin'?

"Now let's say he's got food and he drives back to the house and goes inside. He would hear the phone ringing when he opens the door and he'd run to grab it. He'd think it's Paula finally calling him back. He would've been tryin' to reach her all day and she ain't been home. She'd left that horrible fuckin' message on his phone that morning and he'd be trying to get a hold of her before he has to go away again.

"But suppose the phone call isn't Paula? Suppose it's Mickey Brown, the guy he's got watching Nicole's house? He'd be calling because the same guy The Juice just told him to watch out for, that Goldman kid, he'd just gone inside her house.

"This would get The Juice angry as shit and you can see why. His kids are there. They're sleepin' in the same house with all that stuff goin' on. That's why he's having her watched in the first place. Because she's done this to him before. That Keith guy. The hairdresser. Marcus. She can't get enough and she's doin' it in front of his kids and then lyin' to him about it. He wouldn't know half this stuff if he didn't have Mickey keeping tabs on her.

"So he would tell Mickey to keep watching and he'd hang up the phone. He'd check what time it was. A little after ten. He's gotta leave for the airport at eleven, 'cuz his flight is at eleven forty-five. He'd know he could make it to Nicole's and back in eight minutes because he's timed it before. He'd check in the drawer and find his knit cap and a pair of gloves. If he touches anything, he wouldn't want to leave his fingerprints on it. He would've already been sort of dressed for his trip. He'd get out of those clothes and throw on dark sweats, but he'd leave on the shoes and socks he had on. It would've been quicker, is the only reason. He'd try Paula one more time when he got in the car, but she still wouldn't be home.

"Now, this part is important, Sam." Damn. He'd said my name. If anyone else ever heard this, I was now referred to on the tape.

"The Juice wouldn't be goin' over there to kill *anybody*. The only reason he would take a hat and gloves with him is because he knows if she sees him outside watching her again, she'll probably call the cops. She said she would. So he'd want to make it hard for her to see him and he'd want to be sure if he accidentally touches anything, nobody could prove he was there."

My first thought was, *But if he—you—were just there the night before, your fingerprints would still be all over the house. Why did it matter if you wore gloves the next night?* Then it occurred to me he might actually think the police had equipment sophisticated enough to determine the precise date on which a set of fingerprints had been left. He was wrong, but that didn't matter if he believed it. It would explain the gloves. So I said nothing.

"Now let's say The Juice would get in the Bronco and drive

over there. It would be about ten-fifteen. He'd know where Mickey was parked, across the street on Bundy, and he'd pull up alongside him. Mickey would roll down the window and The Juice would tell him, 'I'll take over from here. You can go home.' Mickey would leave and The Juice would pull around back, into the alleyway. He'd unscrew the little lightbulb that goes on when you open the car door so nobody would see him going in and out. Then he'd unlock the back gate. He would've made sure he always had a key to her place, even if she didn't want him to have one. They're *his* kids living there, too. He'd walk around the side of the condo to the front, where he could see in the window. He'd sort of be in the bushes, so with the dark cap on, it would be hard for her to see him.

"She and Goldman would probably be sitting on the couch. They wouldn't look like they was doin' nothin', but he would know how Nicole works. He'd be able to tell she was putting the moves on him. She would've had candles going and music, and she'd be acting all romantic. She'd still be wearing that same black dress she had on at the recital. The Juice would see all this through the window, even though he wouldn't be able to make out what they were sayin' because of the music.

"After about five or ten minutes of this, let's say Goldman gets up and he acts like he's gonna leave. Nicole wouldn't get up. She'd pull him down toward her and she'd give him this deep tongue kiss. Goldman would stand up again, but he'd be smilin' now, like he's had a good time. She would walk him to the front door.

"The Juice would have moved around so he was inside the

front gate. He would know he's got to stay very still when the door opens, but he's done that before. After a few seconds Goldman would walk out and walk right past him. She'd say something like 'Call me tomorrow, okay?' He'd tell her he would and then he'd go out the gate and start walkin' away. She'd stand there for a minute watchin' him leave.

''Nicole would start to go back in, then he'd hear her say, 'Damn, he forgot to give me the glasses.' She'd turn around and go back down the steps quick, probably trying to catch up with Goldman.

''The Juice would be so close now, he could touch her if he wanted to. But he wouldn't try. He would know how to scare her even more than that. He'd reach into his pocket and he'd pull out his Swiss army knife. He would silently open the blade and lock it at the same time as she was calling, 'Ron! Ron!' Goldman would've had too much of a head start, so he wouldn't hear her. She'd turn around and walk right by him again, only this time, as soon as she'd gone past him, he would jump out at her with the knife. The Juice would be the only one in the world who'd know how much she hated knives, so he'd also know this would scare the shit out of her.

''She'd be at the top of the steps when she saw him. She wouldn't scream. All she would say . . . real quiet, not yelling or anything . . . would be, 'You're pitiful. I'm calling the police. Now they'll finally see how sick you are.' Then she'd turn her back on him and start to go into the house.

''She shouldn't have turned her back on him, man. At this point he'd have to do anything he could to stop her. She'd call the police and try to have The Juice arrested. He couldn't let that happen.

"He'd have to keep her from going inside. He'd have the knife open, but he still wouldn't want to use it. He'd clock her on the back of the head with his fist and she'd go down. She'd be on her knees and she'd kinda look surprised, like she couldn't believe it. She'd start grabbing at him and that's when she would get cut . . . it would be on her hands. He'd push her down the steps and this time she would go down hard. She'd be makin' these sounds, it wouldn't be crying, it'd be like moaning, and the dog would come running over to her.

"Then he would hear footsteps coming up the walk and somebody yelling 'Hey! Hey! Hey!' It would be Goldman and he'd start to come at The Juice, like he thinks he can knock him down. The Juice would sidestep him and Goldman would sorta bounce off him and The Juice would turn and shove Goldman up against the fence with the knife. Goldman would get cut in the stomach, he'd be bleedin', but he'd still keep trying to get the knife away. The Juice would have him pinned against the fence so no matter what he does, Goldman would just cut himself more. But he'd pull the glove off, which is how The Juice would get cut. Goldman finally goes down and then The Juice would see that he's got a big cut on his own hand, real deep, the kind that would hurt like a motherfucker. Then he'd hear Nicole still moaning in front of the gate.

"You gotta understand what would be happening in The Juice's head right now. He'd have to figure that Goldman is dying or dead. He'd know that Nicole won't ever cover for him on something like this. His hand would be killing him, and he'd want to get out of there, but he would also know if he leaves her there like that, she wouldn't keep quiet about it. She would never shut up about any of this. He couldn't have her bad-mouthin' him to the whole world. He's The Juice.

"Then it would get real clear to him, what he's got to do. He would know exactly *how* to do it, too, because he'd just played a navy frogman for this TV pilot and they'd taught him all the ways to use a knife. The navy guy who taught him even said to him, 'Juice, you're getting too good at this.' "

At this point Simpson's voice grew thick with emotion.

"Then . . . well, then he would walk over to her and . . . she's still moaning, she'd be starting to cry, too . . . and he would put his foot in the middle of her back and then he'd pull her hair so tight her head would come all the way up . . . and then he . . . then he would tell her he's sorry that she didn't leave him no choice . . . and then he would do what they taught him how to do.''

Chapter sixteen

"Turn that thing off," said Simpson.

"What . . . ?"

"Sam, turn off the *machine*."

"Oh . . . right. Sure." Until he spoke my name, it hadn't even registered that he was talking to me.

"I've gotta get some water. Just a minute."

He got up out of the swing and walked over to the side of the building where they'd installed a porcelain water fountain for the kids. For a long minute he was bent low, taking swallow after swallow.

As I watched him, my mind struggled to absorb the full import of what he'd just told me. The immediate and overwhelming reaction I had was if he'd really murdered two human beings so savagely—and if he still possessed even the slenderest thread of conscience—he would have killed himself by now.

How could he not? How could he look at those two children even for a moment without constantly realizing he was the sole reason they had no mother? I simply couldn't fathom how he'd be able to function with that knowledge.

Unless, of course, he'd actually convinced himself of his innocence. What was that called in psychiatric terms? A fugue state? It's the state of mind that results from an overload of cognitive dissonance. If someone acts in a way so entirely antithetical to his previous self-image (or, in his case, public image), he literally doesn't remember his own actions. I knew it was rare, but not unprecedented. The mind works to protect itself from something it can't handle. As time elapses, the self-protective memory inevitably becomes the reality. I wondered if he were to take a lie-detector test now, this far removed from the murders, could he pass it?

As he walked back to me I considered the only remaining possibility: he *was* innocent and the whole story was an act. After years of hearings, depositions, and two trials' worth of testimony, he knew, better than anyone, the times, dates, facts, and key figures of these crimes. If he'd chosen to create this scenario for Goldman's benefit—and his own—he was unquestionably the perfect person to write the script.

It worked all three ways. Under the constitutional protection against double jeopardy, he could never again be tried in criminal court for these murders. If he was guilty and he knew it, he'd have no hesitation now about telling the truth—especially if there was a financial incentive as large as the one Goldman was offering.

A Work of Fiction

If he was guilty and honestly didn't know it anymore, or if he really was innocent, then this "confession" was certainly something he was capable of inventing for the money.

"So, whaddaya think, Sam? Think Goldman will buy it?"

"I don't know. I don't really care. I'm not even sure what I should be saying to you right now."

"Hey. Look at me. I'm the same guy I was a minute ago. It's just me, O.J. I told you a story, man. Don't go gettin' crazy on me. I'm makin' all this up, remember?"

"Right. That's what you said." My tone was completely flat. It was meant to convey deep skepticism.

"So you think what I was telling you was true?"

"Wasn't it?" I looked right at him.

The mask was as impenetrable as I'd ever seen it. His eyes were opaque pockets that took in light, but gave none back. As they say in football, he was wearing his "game face."

"No."

As soon as he said this, the mask fell away. His face was open and he was smiling with what appeared to be genuine warmth. Simpson's eyes had now become windows to his vulnerability. For a moment I thought I saw the "real" O.J.—the one who needed to persuade me he was telling the truth because it *was* the truth.

It was impossible not to be affected by the full treatment of O. J. Simpson, even though I knew all of this was just for my benefit. I looked away from him, shaking my head to clear it.

"C'mon, Sam. It's just like Fuhrman. It's a scenario. This is all role-playing, just like you said."

The Confession of O.J. Simpson

Hey, and in a couple of weeks I'm gonna say I made the whole thing up anyway. That'll be something to watch,'' he said, a bitter edge creeping into his voice. ''When I give them this confession, all those people who think they're so fair, so *unbiased*—they're gonna be the ones jumpin' up and down sayin' 'I knew it all along.' Because, no matter what they said, from day one they always *believed* I was guilty.''

Suddenly, he veered sharply from self-pity into self-satisfaction.

''Boy, it's really gonna burn their ass when I say I made it all up.'' He seemed almost gleeful as he pictured it. ''Then they won't know what to believe anymore.''

He was standing on the bottom rung of the jungle gym, his arms and head stuck through the openings. He looked like Gulliver in a Lilliputian jail.

''All right, O.J., whatever you say. Are we done, then?''

He said, ''We oughtta give Fred the whole story, if he's paying for it. Is there more room on the tape?''

I looked at the microcassette. He'd only used about half of it so far. I nodded.

''Okay, come stand over here and turn it back on. Let's do the rest.''

I walked over to the jungle gym and switched the recorder back on.

''So here's the way the rest of it would've happened.

''The goddamn dog would be whining and barking and he wouldn't shut up. The Juice would be breathing too hard now, but he couldn't stop to rest. He would have to get out of there. Fast.

"He'd get back in the car and try to get home as quick as he could. He'd want to make that plane to Chicago. He would think everything would turn out all right somehow if he could only make it on that plane.

"For one thing, he'd be out of town when the police came looking for him. They'd be thrown by that. And nobody else would know he'd even been to Nicole's. Except Mickey. Mickey would know, but that would be all right. He could trust Mickey. Hell, they'd grown up together. He'd known him his whole life. He'd pay him, too. Pay him big time. Mickey would take the money. He'd go along with whatever The Juice needed him to do.

"The Juice would look at his watch and it would be about ten forty-five. He would think if he hurried, he might get lucky and make it home before the limo got there. He'd be driving so fast now that he would almost hit some woman driver at Bundy and San Vicente. Then he'd turn onto his block, onto Rockingham, and when he got close enough to his house, he would see the limo on Ashford. He'd be thinkin', 'Shit. This would be the one night he'd be *early*.'

"The Juice would've figured out to cut his motor and lights and coast to a stop on the Rockingham side. He'd also know not to open the gate, or the driver would see him for sure. So he'd go over to his neighbor's house and he'd get onto his property from there. Just like everybody said at the trial, The Juice would've bumped into Kato's air conditioner in the dark. And he would've dropped the glove back there, too. He'd figure that he'd have plenty of time to go back for it. He just wouldn't have counted on anyone going back there before he got home from Chicago.

"If The Juice was doin' this, he'd get out of his sweats in the bathroom, where he could clean himself up. He'd probably still be bleedin' pretty bad from that cut on his finger. He'd find his round travel bag and he'd stick the sweats and shoes and the pocket knife in there. He wouldn't even notice the blood on the socks. Shit, it took the LAPD weeks to notice anything on 'em. Why couldn't he miss it, too?

"Then he would go downstairs and let the limo guy in. He wouldn't let the limo guy or Kato touch that travel bag.

"When he got to the airport he'd know he'd have to get rid of that travel bag before he could get on the plane. It's got the sweatsuit and the shoes and the knife. He would take it out of the trunk and walk over to the trash can by the curb. People would be watchin' him—they're always watchin' The Juice—so he'd have to be very careful. He would put the bag on top of the trash can and he'd open it. He'd make it seem like he was lookin' for something. The limo driver would be handing the golf clubs to the curbside guy, so he'd be distracted. Here's where The Juice would have to work quick. He'd shove the whole bag deep down into the trash, then he'd pull his hand back out again real fast.

"The only problem would be that all of a sudden he'd re-member they had all this extra security at the airport now because of all the terrorists and shit, and he'd heard somewhere they were going around and checking all the trash cans for metal. He wouldn't want to take a chance they'd find the bag just because it had metal in it, so he'd reach back in to the trash, stick his hand in the bag, and he'd fish out the knife and put it *back* in his pocket. By now, somebody probably would've seen him with his arm all the way in the trash can, but it wouldn't matter because they couldn't see the knife in his hand . . . it was too small when it was closed.

"He would've only had about ten minutes to make his plane now, and even running, it takes three minutes to get to the gate. He'd tell the limo driver to leave, and as soon as he got inside the terminal, he'd go right to a pay phone. There would be only time for one call and he couldn't make it from the plane. He'd dial the number and he would hope that Mickey was home by now. He'd be in luck. He'd say, 'Mickey, it's The Juice. A lot of shit is about to go down and I need you to help me.' Mickey would say, 'Sure, Juice, whatever you need. You know that.' Then The Juice would say, 'Listen to me carefully. There's a big trash can right next to the American Airlines terminal, that's number four, right next to where the guy does the curbside check-in, you know on the top level. You got that so far?' Mickey would say, 'I've got it, Juice.' The Juice would say something like, 'I'm getting on a plane in five minutes. Come out to the airport, right now, and dig in that trash can. You should find my black travel bag with some clothes and shoes in it. Grab it and take it home with you. I'll call you from Chicago, okay?' Mickey would say, 'I'm on top of it right now. It'll take me about forty-five minutes to get to the airport, but I can leave right now.' The Juice'd say, 'Get here as quick as you can, before they empty it, okay? It's real important, man. I gotta go. I'll call you from Chicago in about four hours.' Then he'd hang up and run to the plane. The knife would still be in his pocket when he reached the metal detector, but he wouldn't be worried about it. He'd just take it out, along with his keys and change, and he'd drop everything in that little plastic thing you hand the guy before you walk through the detector. If you're The Juice, you've done this a million times and it's always the same. They're looking at *him,* not at some little red pocketknife. It's got a *corkscrew* in it, they don't give a shit. All they do is say something like 'Keep runnin', Juice,' or 'You gonna make your plane, Juice?' Or their favorite one, 'You got your Hertz car, Juice?' That'd be the way it would happen. He'd be the last one on the plane and everybody'd be making cracks and smilin'. 'It's The Juice. He's always late.'

''He'd stay awake all night on the plane. No way he could sleep. When he landed in Chicago, the Hertz guy would meet him, and while they were waiting for his golf clubs, The Juice would go off to a pay phone and call Mickey, collect. Mickey would have found the bag and brought it home. He also would've seen what was in it. He'd ask The Juice what went down. The Juice would say something like, 'You'll find out. You'll be hearing about it real soon.' Then he'd say, 'Look, Mickey, I'm sorry I got you messed up in this shit, but I'm gonna take care of you, okay? You just gotta lose that bag. Lose it someplace where nobody can ever find it, you understand what I'm sayin'? And here's the deal, if it never turns up, you'll get ten grand every month for the rest of your life, tax-free.' Mickey wouldn't answer him right away, so The Juice would keep talkin'. He'd say, 'You gotta remember, Mick. If somethin' happens to The Juice, there's no money left for anybody.' Mickey would've said, 'I hear you, Juice.' And somebody as good as Mickey, he would've made that bag disappear completely.

"He would've made himself disappear, too, until everything blew over."

I thought, if there really was a "Mickey," at least he would have left a forwarding address. The one thing he'd want catching up with him would be those ten-thousand-dollar checks every month.

"You think Goldman needs much more than this to make him happy, Sam?"

I clicked off the recorder. It was irrational, but I still felt by keeping my voice off the tape, I could protect some part of me that didn't want to be involved in this.

"I don't know Fred Goldman. He's lost his son. He wants to hear you admit that you did it. I guess you've done that now. Any more details are up to you, I suppose."

"Well, let's see. There is one more detail we could give him. I've been thinkin' about whether I wanted to go with this part of the story, but what the hell."

I turned the tape recorder on again.

"Everybody wants to know where the knife went. Well, here's what could've happened. After The Juice takes the knife to Chicago, he would've kept it in his pocket. Truth is, he probably wouldn't have thought about it no more. He'd already wiped it clean, so it was just his pocketknife again. Lots of people got pocketknives with 'em all the time, right?

"So he'd bring it back from Chicago and he would've had it with him when he got to his house. It would've been in his pocket when they handcuffed him. Then, when they let him go and said they needed to take his statement downtown, he *still* would have had it on him. See, he wouldn't have even been thinkin' about it. It was a pocketknife. It was totally clean, so he wouldn't be worried about it. There might've been a moment down at the police station when he'd have thought, 'I've got this pocketknife and I'm goin' through a metal detector. What if they stop me?' But, you know what? It would turn out to be the same thing as the airport, he'd take it out and they'd just give it back to him. They were all lookin' for some big *Psycho* kinda knife, not some dinky Swiss army job with a corkscrew.

"And he would've still had that knife in his pocket two days later down in Laguna when he went to say good-bye to Nicole. They had her all fixed up . . . she was really beautiful . . . and there were all these white flowers around her, like they were some kind of bed for her to sleep in."

He was talking quietly now, remembering how she looked the last time he would ever see her.

"He would've wanted some time alone with her. Judy and the family would've gone into the other room. He would've cried and told her he loved her too much. And then he would've taken the pocketknife out and placed it in the bed of flowers with her. That's the way The Juice would've done it."

182

CHAPTER SEVENTEEN

It was a short drive home from Potrero Hill. Simpson spent the whole ride looking out the window, humming tunelessly. I couldn't get his story out of my head. Words and phrases kept repeating themselves, as though he were saying them again out loud.

"He'd know he'd have to get rid of that travel bag before he could get on the plane. . . . They're lookin' at him not at some little red pocketknife. . . . He couldn't have her bad-mouthin' him to the whole world. He's The Juice. . . . She shouldn't have turned her back on him, man. . . . That's what The Juice would've done."

We got back to my house at about nine-thirty. Before he left, we stood for a minute by my car.

"I've got to go back to my mom's place and get my clothes. Do you think you can write up that paper?"

183

The Confession of O. J. Simpson

I answered the form if not the substance of his question. "You've certainly given me enough material," I said.

He either didn't notice, or chose not to acknowledge, my lawyerly nuance.

"Great. It should take me about an hour to pack everything and meet you back here."

"Okay," I said, not really sure if it was, but relieved to finally see him get into his car and drive away.

I walked into my house, and for a moment it felt unfamiliar to me. So much had happened in so brief a span that I felt as if I was walking back into my life after having been away a long time. I went upstairs to my office.

Sitting down at my desk, I lit a cigarette, and noticed the hand holding the match wasn't steady. On the rare occasions when I smoked, I would always open a window for ventilation. Today I just sat there, immobile, the smoke billowing around my head.

No matter how thick the smoke, it couldn't obscure the images I now had of Nicole Brown and Ron Goldman. What Simpson had described was as vivid as if I'd been there myself. If he'd woven it all as a fantasy from his own imagination, then he was the greatest storyteller I'd ever encountered. If, as seemed infinitely more likely, he was remembering the events as they'd happened, then I was faced with the dilemma of what I could or should do with this awful knowledge.

Technically, I was under no obligation to do anything. I was his attorney; he was my client. If this story was true, then he had definitely committed perjury in both his deposition and testimony at the civil trial. He'd made it clear to me yesterday (was it only yesterday?) that he was prepared to take the risk of being prosecuted on a perjury charge, if it meant Goldman would waive the judgment against him. And if in fact he had committed perjury, he'd done so long before he'd come to me, therefore nothing I did would be suborning him to it.

Now, as I looked down at the legal pad on my desk which still bore the heading *Simpson: Confession,* I was confronted with the decision every attorney deals with at some point in his or her professional life. Many reconcile it early on, some wrestle with it for an entire career. If I believed him to be guilty, should I give him any help at all?

The confession he wanted me to draft was not, in and of itself, a crime. He was also holding open the possibility of later repudiating his statement in order to resurrect what might remain of his public image. The contract he'd asked me to draft for Goldman would be structured to stand up in court even in the event he recanted. This, too, was not technically a crime, so long as he fulfilled his contractual obligation to Fred Goldman. He would make a complete public statement of his guilt and then he'd pay for its publication in major newspapers. If he was never required to swear to the veracity of the statement, then, legally, I could help him do all of this.

But this was no longer a legal issue. In law school, I'd been taught a well-defined canon of ethical conduct for attorneys. Nothing like this was included in my course of study. Here again—as Rachel had described it angrily so many times during our marriage—I was paralyzed with an attack of ethics.

However, this situation was completely different from helping Melvin Belli win yet another dubious personal-injury case.

I decided to take a shower. I turned the water on as hot as I could stand it and let it run for a long time. Immediately, my mind returned to the question of what I would do next.

Why don't you get down from your high horse? I suddenly thought. *This holier-than-thou attitude of yours has brought your family nothing but misery. Arguably it wrecked your marriage. For once, why don't you look at the reality of something? All the damage has already been done. All of your hand-wringing won't bring Nicole Simpson or Ron Goldman back to life. You want to be able to provide for Laura and guarantee her future. Fred Goldman wants peace of mind and you can help him get that. O. J. Simpson wants thirteen million dollars and he says he's willing to put it in trust for his children. It's hard to see that as a selfish act. If he tries to recant, you always have the option of doing what Kardashian did: going public with the truth. C'mon, Sam. This should be a no-brainer.*

When I got out of the shower, I knew what I intended to do. I tied the towel around my waist and walked back into the office. This journal lay open on my desk and the microcassettes were still stacked neatly on top of the answering machine. I put the tapes back into the pouch and zipped it up. I took all the papers and letters and folded them carefully so they would fit easily into the leather binder. This done, I put the binder in the bottom drawer of my filing cabinet, the one that locked. I removed the tape recorder from my pocket and put that in the drawer as well.

Then I went back to my desk and wrote out O. J. Simpson's confession on the yellow pad.

Just as I finished I heard Laura's voice calling from downstairs.

"Dad, are you home?"

"I'm just getting out of the shower, sweetheart. Give me a minute and I'll be right down."

I grabbed my checkbook off the desk and went into the bedroom. This isn't going to be a casual day, I thought. I took out my charcoal-gray suit and chose a red power tie to go with it. Dressed, I went downstairs and saw Laura sitting on the couch watching MTV.

Something occurred to me and I asked her, "Have you ever heard of a singer named Courtney Love?"

She looked at me with a curious expression as if to say, 'Are you serious?'

Realizing I was, she said, "Yeah, she's in a band called Hole. They're kind of early nineties. Why?"

I smiled at her. "No reason."

"Don't you have school this morning?" I asked, changing the subject.

"Not till eleven," she replied. "I've got three free periods this morning. You know how it is, Dad. I'm a senior."

"Right. I almost forgot."

She shifted uneasily on the couch and kept her eyes on the TV. "So . . . Mom asked me to come by and—"

"She sent you to pick up the checks, right?" I said this as mildly as I could.

The Confession of O. J. Simpson

"Listen, I don't want to get into the middle of this, Dad. I told her I'd come by and pick them up if you had them. It's okay if you don't. That's between you and her."

I took the checkbook out of my suit pocket and wrote out both checks. She watched me do this and looked greatly relieved when I handed them to her.

"That's great. Thank you, Dad. Mom's gonna be so happy. She's under a lot of pressure, you know. . . ."

"I know."

She folded the checks and put them in the pocket of her backpack. She was getting ready to leave.

"So, Dad, I want to apologize for what I said to you yesterday about Simpson. I didn't mean to hurt your feelings or anything. It kind of took me by surprise, him being here."

"That's okay, sweetheart. I understand. It was strange for me, too, having him here."

"What happened to him?" she asked, standing in the doorway.

"He agreed to pay me for my time and he went home." Another lawyer's answer, I thought sardonically.

"So, did he take your advice?" she asked.

"I don't know, sweetheart. I haven't really given it to him yet."

She looked at me for a moment without speaking, then she said, with all the seriousness of her age, "I know whatever you tell him to do, you'll think about it very carefully. And it will be the right thing."

She kissed me on the cheek and I held her for a moment,

wordlessly acknowledging her vote of confidence. God, I loved her.

I stared at her a moment as she walked away, then I closed the door and went back inside.

Simpson returned a little after eleven o'clock. When I let him in, I noticed he had also changed. The polo shirt and khakis were gone, replaced by a dark sport coat, white dress shirt, and tailored dress slacks.

He looked at me with a grin and said, "You clean up real nice, Sam."

I said, "Thanks. Come on in."

He followed me up to my office. When I sat down at my desk, with him once again sitting opposite me, I experienced a powerful sense of déjà vu. I handed him the yellow legal pad. It was no longer blank. Under the words *Simpson: Confession* I had written three pages of his admission of guilt.

It took him a long time to read it. When he was done he looked up at me and said, "I guess this says it."

I said, "Well, let's see if Fred Goldman thinks so. If you're willing to sign it, then I'll go ahead and print it out. I still have to prepare the document that says he'll waive the judgment against you in return for your publicly issuing this statement. That should take me another couple of hours."

"That sounds great, Sam. Maybe I'll go grab us some lunch while you do that." He was getting up out of the chair.

I said, "Wait a minute. I should call Petrocelli now and see if he's in or if they're even willing to meet with us."

"Okay," said Simpson. "Go ahead."

I'd written down Petrocelli's number earlier. Now I punched it into the phone.

"Mitchell, Silberberg and Knupp," said the receptionist.

"Daniel Petrocelli's office, please."

A moment later another voice said, "Mr. Petrocelli's office. May I help you?"

I said, "It's Samuel Roosevelt. Is he in?"

"Just a moment, Mr. Roosevelt. Will he know what this is regarding?"

"Tell him I'm representing . . ." I paused for a moment. I was about to say it to someone else for the first time. "Tell him I'm representing O. J. Simpson on a matter relating to the Goldman action."

"Just a moment, Mr. Roosevelt. I'll see if he can talk to you."

After a moment Daniel Petrocelli came on the line. I'd never met him, but I'd seen him interviewed. I'd been impressed with the way he'd handled the Goldman civil case and even more so with how he conducted himself in the media. I was formal, but friendly.

"Mr. Petrocelli, I'm Samuel Roosevelt. I'm an attorney representing O. J. Simpson with respect to your client's civil action."

"Go ahead," said Petrocelli.

He was probably thinking, Jesus, he's got *another* attorney. I took a breath.

"Mr. Simpson is prepared to meet your client's request for

a statement about his culpability in the criminal matter. I'm drafting that statement right now.''

There was a long silence on Petrocelli's end of the line. When he spoke, finally, his voice betrayed his skepticism.

''Let me see if I understand what you're saying to me, Mr. Roosevelt. Your client is ready to provide a statement admitting to the murders of Ronald Goldman and Nicole Brown. Is that what you're saying?''

''Yes,'' I replied. ''And he's prepared to make that statement publicly, just as Mr. Goldman has requested. In return, he wants a full waiver of the civil judgment your client is holding against him. Again, this is per your client's public request of Mr. Simpson.''

Another long silence.

''I'm going to have to call my client and call you back. Where can I reach you, Mr. Roosevelt?''

I gave him my number and he said he'd get back to me within thirty minutes.

I told Simpson we had to wait and I began drafting the second document.

Ten minutes later Petrocelli was back on the line.

''My client is prepared to discuss this. When can you meet?''

I said, ''Mr. Simpson is here in San Francisco right now. We can take the shuttle this afternoon and be in your office by late today. Would that work for you and your client?''

He replied quickly. ''Four o'clock.''

The Confession of O. J. Simpson

I said, "We'll be there."

When I hung up Simpson was wearing his Cheshire grin. "They went for it," he said.

"We'll see. We're due there at four o'clock. I've got to finish this agreement. Why don't you go get us some lunch?"

Three hours later we were in my car speeding toward the airport. The shuttle flight was at two-thirty and we barely had enough time to make it.

We parked my car in the short-term lot at 2:23 P.M. and ran into the terminal.

Simpson set the pace and I struggled to keep up with it. We got to the metal detectors at 2:26 P.M. The security attendant recognized Simpson and it was just as he described it to me.

"Running late, O.J.?" The man was grinning like he'd said something particularly clever.

"You know it." Simpson returned the smile, and for a moment he was the old O.J.—not a care in the world, except for making his plane.

"Hope you got your Hertz car!" the man called after us as we ran down to the gate.

We made it onto the plane with one minute to spare, just as the doors were closing behind us.

Simpson's reception on the plane was in stark contrast to what he'd received from the man at the metal detector. The stewardess was curt.

"You have to take your seats immediately, we're about to take off." Walking behind him down the aisle, I could tell many of the passengers were deliberately averting their eyes as he passed by. It was as if eye contact with him might signify some sort of approval. If he noticed any of this, he didn't let on.

The flight to Los Angeles took a little over an hour. He spent most of it staring out the window. I reviewed the two documents, checking for any serious mistakes. Given the speed with which I'd drafted them, I was surprised not to find anything that needed changing.

We took a cab to Petrocelli's office in West Los Angeles. Ironically, I noticed the exit the driver took getting off the freeway was Bundy Drive.

Petrocelli's secretary led us into a conference room and then closed the door behind her as she left. Simpson and I sat in the last two chairs along one side of a long conference table.

In a moment the door opened again and Petrocelli entered, followed by Fred and Kim Goldman.

"Uh-uh. No way." Simpson was out of his chair. "Not her."

Kim Goldman was quick and sharp in her response.

"What's the matter, *killer*? Are you still afraid of me?" Her voice was dripping with sarcasm, but even from across the room I could see she was shaking with rage.

I introduced myself to Petrocelli.

"I'm Sam Roosevelt. We spoke on the phone." Petrocelli shook my hand, but when I extended it to Goldman, he ignored me. He was addressing Simpson.

"Listen, you animal. You kept her out of the deposition. She has every right to be here now."

"Sam, you tell him if she stays, we're out of here."

Petrocelli brought everything to a halt. Quietly, he said, "Kim, let's do this. Your father and I will listen to what they have to say, and before anything is agreed to, we'll come out and talk together in my office. How's that?" His tone was direct, yet compassionate.

She glared at Simpson, but nodded in acquiescence to Petrocelli's plan.

When she'd left the room, Goldman and Petrocelli sat down together on our side but nearer the middle of the conference table. It was apparent they'd been through this with Simpson before and had no intention of sitting closer to him.

Goldman's gaze was riveted on Simpson. Simpson looked away.

I stood up and passed two copies of both Simpson's statement and the waiver to Petrocelli. He handed one of each to Goldman and they both began reading.

I stopped them. "You understand that Mr. Goldman must agree to sign the waiver of the judgment if he accepts Mr. Simpson's statement?"

Petrocelli said nothing. Goldman's eyes burned holes into mine. I sat down.

Petrocelli finished first and waited for Goldman. His client was staring at Simpson's statement intently. Did he think if he stopped reading the words, they might disappear? Finally, he took off his glasses and wiped his eyes.

Petrocelli spoke first. "Fred, why don't we go into my office now and discuss this with Kim?"

I interjected. "I need to tell you my client's position on this. It's a onetime offer. If Mr. Goldman chooses not to sign the waiver now, he intends to take it off the table."

Petrocelli was suddenly furious.

"That is unacceptable!" He was out of his chair. "We're not signing anything without taking time to review it. I can guarantee you that."

Goldman wasn't looking at Simpson anymore. He was still looking at the document in his hand. When he spoke, his voice was odd. It sounded distant.

"I'll sign. Give me the paper."

"Fred, listen to me. You can't. . . ."

Goldman looked at me. He'd found his voice again. "Give me the goddamned paper!" he shouted.

I took the waiver agreement out of my briefcase and passed it down the table to Goldman. He took out his pen and signed it. Petrocelli was shaking his head in disbelief.

When he finished signing it, Goldman took the pen and, with considerable force, threw it right at Simpson's head. Simpson flinched, but then picked the pen up off the floor and, without a word, signed the copy of his confession I'd placed in front of him. He handed it to me and started to get out of his chair, as if to leave. I stood up with him.

Suddenly he was frozen in place, staring past me. When I turned to see what he was looking at, I saw Fred Goldman had also risen from his chair. He was pointing a gun directly at Simpson.

CHAPTER EIGHTEEN

Each of the next thirty seconds became a separate and distinct measure of time.

I felt like I was seeing everything from above the room, the same perspective attributed to someone having a near-death experience. My senses all seemed heightened, keener. I heard the ticking of Petrocelli's wristwatch. I saw an individual bead of perspiration form just above Simpson's right temple. My right hand felt the coldness of Goldman's gun as if I was holding it myself. I could even taste the sweet metallic flavor of the adrenaline each of us was pumping at near-toxic levels.

Simpson and I were both standing about six feet away from Goldman. Petrocelli was still sitting in his chair next to Goldman. Of the two, Goldman was closer to us.

Since the conference room had no windows, and the one door next to Goldman was closed as soon as we came in, none of the firm's other lawyers or staff could observe what was taking place.

Simpson, who still had the pen in his hand, was no longer avoiding Goldman's stare. Strangely, he was now returning it with a half smile, as if he found Goldman amusing or not really serious.

Goldman's seriousness of purpose was underscored by the sound of the trigger being pulled back, followed by the sound of the gun cocking.

Petrocelli was out of his chair, shouting, "Fred! No!"

Goldman didn't take his eyes off Simpson, but said, with calm intensity, "Stay out of this, Dan. It's between me and that thing."

I instinctively tried to push Simpson down into his chair. Without looking at me, he easily resisted. His eyes remained locked on Goldman, who began speaking to him.

"I want you to *beg*, you animal. Beg for that worthless life that's so goddamned precious to you. Go ahead, I'm giving you more of a chance than you gave Ronnie."

"Fred, you can't . . . he's not worth it. . . ." Petrocelli wasn't speaking to his client anymore; he was imploring a friend.

For only an instant Fred Goldman looked at Petrocelli.

Simpson saw his opening and took it. He rushed Goldman with the full force of his weight, carrying them both into the far wall of the conference room. Goldman's glasses went flying across the table and I thought, wildly, *They're going to break.*

The sharp pop of the revolver echoed briefly in the

rectangular room, muffled only by the two-hundred-pound weight that had set it off.

Simpson slumped to the floor in front of Goldman, who looked dazed. The conference-room door flew open and Kim Goldman ran to her father. Petrocelli was already on the phone to 911, even as the doorway became crowded with people hoping to catch a glimpse of this soon-to-be historic tableau.

I was the first one—the only one—who went to Simpson. His eyes had rolled back in his head and he was bleeding profusely from a wound in his upper abdomen.

Be careful what you wish for, I thought as the paramedics arrived with his stretcher.

CHAPTER NINETEEN

The media encampment outside Saint John's Hospital in Santa Monica was now in its third day. The hospital parking lot had virtually become a tent city for the international press corps, whose numbers and intensity far surpassed even that of Simpson's criminal trial.

This was *O. J. Simpson: The Deathwatch.*

In fact, each network had created what it hoped was an evocative title to "personalize" its own coverage of the vigil. Peter Jennings and ABC were providing round-the-clock reports of Simpson's condition under the banner headline *Life in the Balance.* NBC, CNBC, and MSNBC were all grouped together under the umbrella of *O. J. Simpson: Fighting for Life.* (In an unfortunate coincidence, CBS had chosen to go with the very similar *Simpson's Fight for Life,* which prompted a nasty on-air exchange between Dan Rather and Tom Brokaw over whose title came first.) Fox, possibly with an eye toward cross-promotion with its sponsorship of the NFL, had chosen to pose the question *O.J.'s Final Run?* CNN anchor Bernard Shaw gravely intoned his comments with THE WORLD STANDS VIGIL superimposed over him on the screen. This international spin presumably reflected CNN's sensitivity to its global affiliates.

From the first few minutes of Simpson's arrival, the sidewalks of Santa Monica Boulevard were overrun with spectators. The crowds tripled every hour until the police were finally forced to cordon off a square mile area surrounding the hospital. Far from causing them to disperse, this meant only that the crowds were now massing outside of the security perimeter. Much of Santa Monica had become impassable due to the sheer volume of humanity that had descended on this beach community. "Simpstock," some people were calling it. Only instead of music and love, the air was filled with shouts and epithets. "Pull the plug!" someone shouted. One woman was screaming "Hitler was right!" at anybody who looked even vaguely Semitic.

Mass-produced signs and buttons were already being sold to willing buyers on either side of the emotional divide. FRY FRED was a very popular button, as was a bumper sticker that said PRAY FOR THE JUICE. The most popular anti-Simpson item was a T-shirt that subtly read GOOD on the front and RIDDANCE on the back. Most bizarre of all were the rubber Simpson masks, left over from Halloween, being worn by people on both sides. Those who were pro-Simpson were dressing up in white garb, perhaps suggesting an angelic O.J. The Simpson haters used ketchup on the masks to make their own, particularly morbid, statement.

The real Simpson was in critical condition. He had suffered massive internal bleeding from a single shot that entered his upper abdominal cavity and caused considerable damage before exiting through his left shoulder blade. His prognosis was not good. Since being brought to the hospital, he'd been in and out of consciousness. In the few times he'd been awake, his doctors said he was disoriented and his speech was garbled and incomprehensible. It seemed highly unlikely he would be able to answer any questions, including those of the police, who wanted very much to take his statement.

I was included in a small group of Simpson's family and close friends who were gathered on the hospital's second floor, outside the intensive-care unit where Simpson was being kept in isolation and under heavy guard. Since the shooting, I had been staying in a nearby motel, shuttling back and forth between the hospital, police headquarters, and the district attorney's office. Goldman had been immediately arrested and charged with attempted murder. He was being held, without bail, in the Santa Monica jail. My statement, along with Petrocelli's, had served to reduce the charge against Goldman to attempted manslaughter and, that morning, a judge had agreed to set bail for him in the amount of $250,000. His family had announced their intention to post bail and his release was expected by tonight.

Goldman's potential freedom immediately became the hot topic of discussion for the media, which previously had been constrained by events into reporting this only as a medical story. After two days of interviewing doctors, nurses, and even hospital orderlies, and after endlessly rehashing diagrams depicting Simpson's entry and exit wounds in minute and mind-numbing detail, the anchors and reporters were visibly relieved when this story once again took its proper place as a search for "truth." Even before the shooting, the news divisions were already paying high fees to their legal "experts"; none of the networks had the foresight to keep a doctor on retainer. So when Goldman's case took center stage, the networks were finally able to utilize their high-priced stables of legal talent. This generated first a stream, then a torrent, of hyperbole about how the Simpson/Goldman conflict reflected society's ongoing struggle to reconcile the often fundamental differences between legal and moral justice.

Which is what, as Roger Cossack was explaining to Greta van Susteren at that very moment, "this tragic case exemplifies." For a change, I was watching television alone, in the second-floor family waiting room of Saint John's Hospital.

Simpson's family members were taking turns in his room, waiting to see when, or if, he would again regain consciousness.

Although they were polite, Simpson's family and close friends didn't know quite what to make of me. They knew Simpson had been talking with me, but he'd never told them about what. Thus far, his whole "confession" had been kept out of the press, but it was being widely reported that my statement to the authorities had helped reduce the charges against Goldman. This certainly hadn't endeared me to the Simpson clan.

So I was more than a little surprised when Simpson's sister

A Work of Fiction

Shirley came into the room and approached me. We'd exchanged very few words over the previous two days.

"He's awake," she said. "And he's asking for you." She clearly wasn't overjoyed to deliver this message. The first time her brother was able to speak, he wanted to talk to me, the Goldman-lover.

I followed her down the hall, stopping outside of Simpson's room. I held the door open for her, but she stayed back.

"He just wants to see you."

I entered the brightly lit ICU room and saw Simpson, breathing through an oxygen mask. This was the first time I'd seen him since the ambulance had taken him away. He looked pale, but not as bad as I'd expected. His eyes were half-open and he seemed reasonably alert. A doctor and two nurses were hovering over him. The doctor was writing something in the chart. One of the nurses was tending to Simpson's IV, the other was checking his heart rate on an electronic monitor.

The doctor approached me before I could get to Simpson.

She said, "Are you Mr. Roosevelt?"

"Yes."

"This is the first time he's been really coherent. He's very weak, but he insists on seeing you. We're watching him very carefully right now; the next twenty-four hours are critical for him. Please only stay a few minutes. And try not to say or do anything that excites him."

I nodded and walked over to the side of his bed. He looked at me and tried to speak, but the mask prevented it. He tried to move it aside and one of the nurses immediately stopped him.

His eyes flashed with anger at her interference, but he wasn't strong enough to resist. He beckoned me to get closer. I bent my head down next to the mask until I could hear his whispered question.

"What happened?"

I told him. His eyes told me he understood what I was saying to him. I also told him Goldman had been arrested for an attempt on his life. I decided to take the doctor's advice and not mention the charge had already been reduced to manslaughter, just in case that information might somehow agitate him.

He stared at me for a moment, and although his mouth was partially concealed by the oxygen mask, his eyes made it clear he was smiling.

After talking with him for only a few minutes more, I left his room. His family was eager to find out what he'd said, but I could tell them little.

I said, "He's resting some more. He's asked me to do something for him, which I promised I would. The doctor says you should be able to see him when he wakes up again."

This didn't satisfy them at all.

Shirley said, "What is it he wants you to do? It's not about a will, is it?"

"No," I said. "He just wants me to take a message to somebody. Excuse me, I'll be back in a few minutes."

I got out of there before they could ask me any more questions. Passing through security, I took the elevator down to the first floor and exited through the hospital's main entrance.

Immediately, I was surrounded by a wild horde of reporters

feverishly screaming questions at me, most of whom I couldn't understand because they were shouting over one another. I tried to sidestep the boom microphones that were being thrust in front of me, but one of them struck me on the side of the head. Nobody apologized.

"Mr. Roosevelt, how is he?"

"Is he conscious, Sam?"

"We've heard that he's been dead since this morning. Can you confirm that?"

I pushed my way through them, using "no comment" as my only protection.

I managed to get behind the first phalanx of cameras to a clearing where, every ten feet or so, a canvas back director's chair had been set up in front of a single camera. There must have been at least a dozen of these. Each of the network anchors and many of the hosts of newsmagazine shows had established a small territory in the parking lot from which to do his or her nightly "stand-up." It was from that position, using the hospital as a backdrop, that the nation would be given positive proof of Peter, Tom, Dan, Bernie, et al., actually *participating* in "The Vigil of the Century." It wouldn't do to be phoning this one in.

It was in this area that I found the person I was looking for, a mustachioed man with dark, wavy hair and glasses. He was not on-camera at the moment, but he was reading intently from the notes in his hand, as if he was getting ready to go on the air soon.

"You're Geraldo Rivera, right?" I said, approaching him.

He looked up, startled someone would break his concentration. Then he recognized me and said, "I sure am." He was smiling now. "And you're Sam Roosevelt. We're on live in two minutes. Can I get you to come on the air with me, Sam?"

"No, I'm sorry. That's not why I'm here. I'd like to bring you inside with me, if that's okay with you."

If he was surprised by this, he didn't show it. He turned immediately to the man standing next to him and said, "Joe, how much time have we got?"

"A minute forty-five, Geraldo."

"Tell the studio we're throwing it back to them. See if you can get Grodin to go on now. Use videotape if you have to."

Joe started to protest, but Rivera wasn't listening. He removed his earpiece and said, "Let's go."

I said, "Do you have a cameraman you can bring with you?"

He looked at me as if I'd said he'd just won the lottery. In a way, he had.

"You bet I do."

Within a minute the three of us were pushing our way through the crowd of press, all of whom were unhappy to see Rivera leading the way.

"Hey, where are *you* going?"

"If *he's* going in, I'm going in, too."

"This isn't *fair*."

I smiled to myself when I heard that one. Damn right, it's not fair. And now *you* know how it feels.

The guard at the main entrance didn't want to allow Rivera and his cameraman in the door, but the credential I had from the hospital gave me "pull." It allowed me to bring anyone inside as long as they were escorted by me.

The scene on the second floor was more complicated. Simpson's family and friends, particularly Shirley, were horrified to see Geraldo Rivera in their midst.

I walked over to her and said, "This is who he sent me out to get."

She looked at me coldly and said, "I don't believe you."

I said, "Go ahead. Ask him yourself."

She looked first at me, then at Rivera. Finally, she turned and went into her brother's room.

Rivera had suddenly realized he was about to get inside Simpson's room with a camera. To say he was excited by that prospect was an understatement.

He put his arm around my shoulder, drawing me close to him. In an urgent whisper, he said, "You mean Simpson *asked* for me? You heard him?"

I told him he had. Rivera seemed stunned, but more than ready for whatever happened next.

After a few minutes the door opened, and Shirley emerged. Her expression told me that Simpson was awake and had confirmed what I'd told her was true.

She didn't look at us. She just held the door and said, "Go ahead."

Simpson was now slightly more elevated in the bed, and he'd removed his oxygen mask. I assumed there'd been a donnybrook with the nurses over this. They had to make the no-win decision of either forcing him to keep it on, thereby greatly upsetting him, or allowing him to remove it and possibly risking his infection. As usual, Simpson got his way. I couldn't even imagine how he'd persuaded them to allow Rivera and his cameraman inside the room. Upon entering, each of us was immediately given gloves and a surgical mask to put on.

"O.J.," I said, "here's Geraldo Rivera."

"Excuse me for not shaking hands with you, man."

"That's okay, O.J." He was plainly still mystified as to why he was here. He looked at me, and I shrugged, as if to say, "Wait. You'll see."

"Do you have enough light to shoot in here?" Simpson asked.

The lights of the ICU were as powerful as any natural light. Rivera turned to his cameraman, who nodded quickly.

Simpson spoke softly but distinctly. "Go ahead then, turn on the camera, I've got something I want to say." His breathing was plainly labored. One of the nurses tried to get him to put the oxygen mask back on, but he pushed her away.

With the camera rolling, Simpson began to speak. He was looking directly into the lens.

"I want to tell everyone that you shouldn't blame Mr. Goldman for what happened to me. It was an accident . . . not his fault. I hit him and the gun went off. I know he didn't mean to shoot me. Please don't blame him for this. It was an accident. That's it. That's what I wanted to say. You can turn the camera off now."

Rivera stared at Simpson for a moment, then looked at me, dumbfounded.

210

"That's it?" he managed to say.

"That's it," I replied.

One nurse had already put Simpson's oxygen mask back on, and his eyes were closed again, foreclosing the possibility of Rivera asking him any questions. The other nurse was aggressively moving the cameraman out of the ICU, and Rivera, reluctantly, was forced to follow him.

I was still at Simpson's bedside. Before I could move toward the door, Simpson reached up and grabbed my wrist, pulling me down to him.

With effort, but clearly enough so that there could be no mistaking the words, he said, "I wonder if Fred will ever understand what I've just done."

I was certain I could see the half-smile underneath the mask.

CHAPTER TWENTY

Cambridge was still warm in late August. Even though the leaves were beginning to hint at their autumnal intent, the short-shirt-sleeved young women and men in Harvard Square were paying far more attention to one another than they were to the foliage.

Rachel and I, in a well-timed display of harmony, had agreed both of us would accompany Laura when she enrolled for classes. The two of them would be arriving at Logan Airport that afternoon. I'd be picking them up in the rented van that I'd just driven cross-country with Laura's clothes, books, stereo, and computer. Everything could have been shipped, but I'd really wanted the time alone in the car.

The last five months were still barely in focus for me. Simpson was dead. On his fourth day in the hospital, he'd contracted pneumonia. At that point he had no chance of recovery.

The Confession of O.J. Simpson

His funeral became the second ring in that year's media circus. Roosevelt Grier had presided over the memorial service, which, of course, was carried live on every broadcast medium licensed by the FCC.

Johnnie Cochran delivered a stirring eulogy, telling the mourners at First AME Baptist Church that Simpson had died "a hero's death, with sincerity in his heart and forgiveness on his lips. The Lord will welcome him to heaven as his prodigal son returned."

In early summer, a grand jury returned an indictment of involuntary manslaughter against Fred Goldman. The radio call-in shows were flooded with calls from thousands of listeners whose opinions ran the gamut from vengeful ("They should string him up behind the courthouse like they would if he was black and O.J. was white") to the righteous ("O.J. forgave him. Why can't we? God will judge him"). Others believed Goldman was a hero ("Fred should plead guilty and say O.J. was wrong again, he *did* mean to shoot him").

The trial in Santa Monica lasted three days. I testified that I was certain Fred Goldman never intended to pull the trigger.

Goldman's attorney, Gerry Spence, led his client through an emotional retelling of the shooting and of his state of mind at the time.

Even with his freedom on the line, Goldman couldn't refrain from speaking the absolute truth. "I wanted him to feel what Ronnie felt. I wouldn't have shot him. I'm not the murderer. He was. And I'm not sorry he's dead."

The jury, whose ethnic makeup mirrored that of the jury in

the civil trial, took two hours to reach a verdict. The Hispanic foreman, flanked by his colleagues, eleven men and women, all non-Hispanic Caucasians, handed their sealed decision to the court clerk, who read it aloud: "We, the jury, in the above-entitled action, find the defendant, Frederic Goldman, not guilty of the crime of involuntary manslaughter."

Pandemonium erupted in the courtroom. Most of the gallery cheered and applauded, although a few angry spectators shouted "murderer" as the Goldmans exited the courtroom through a rear door. I refused all interviews, but Gerry Spence, resplendent in his buckskin vest outside the courtroom, said exactly what I would have said: "This jury believed one witness: O. J. Simpson."

After the trial, I went home to San Francisco and quickly discovered that I would not be returning to my previous life right away. My testimony about Simpson's intention to recant his confession had prompted a number of questions to the state bar about my involvement in the scheme. Nothing had resulted from it, however, other than a few editorials in the legal newspapers about whether or not I'd behaved improperly.

No one ever asked me if Simpson had recorded his confession. Nor had I volunteered the information. My yellow legal pad and Simpson's signed statement had both been entered into evidence at Goldman's trial. But no one knew about the existence of the tapes or of Simpson's journal.

I was inundated with offers to sell my story. It staggered the mind to consider what price the tapes and journal might bring had I been willing to sell them on the open market. I'd read that one Japanese collector had already offered $500,000 for Goldman's gun and $1,000,000 for Simpson's bloody shirt.

One night, shortly after I'd returned to San Francisco, I was sitting alone in my living room. The night was chilly. No doubt it was the breeze coming off the bay. Even in mid-summer, it wasn't uncommon for me to use my fireplace at night.

The balled-up pages from Simpson's yellow legal pad made good kindling. Each of the little microcassettes made a soft hissing sound when it caught fire.

As the fire died away I sat awhile, staring at the embers. I smiled when I thought what Rachel's reaction would be if I ever told her I'd done this. "Jesus, Sam, couldn't you have saved even *one* little tape? What's wrong with you?" I thought about Simpson's spiritual kinship with Richard Nixon and about how so many people wished that Nixon had done for himself what I'd just done for Simpson.

Had I done it for him? Not really. Finally, Simpson's image didn't matter anymore. All his spinning and manipulating, his posturing and pleading—it was all over and done with for him.

However, there were two people who still could have been deeply affected by the publication of Simpson's journal. If they chose, Sydney and Justin Simpson could still believe that their father died an innocent man. My testimony had provided significant doubt about the truth of his "confession." That doubt, coupled with the tremendous outpouring of sympathy they'd received, might help balance the scales a bit for those kids, who have such a tough road ahead of them.

Now, sitting in my hotel room overlooking Harvard Square,

A Work of Fiction

I remembered seeing a letter Simpson had written to Nicole after their violent New Year's Eve argument, five years before her death:

Nicole:
You know I could never hurt you. You are the person I love most in the world. You know that. Whatever I did, I'm sorry. Please try to find it in your heart to forgive me. I know we have a great future together.

Love,
O.J.

He'd never sent it.

EPILOGUE

Geraldo Rivera's "interview" with O. J. Simpson was the highest rated regularly scheduled program in the history of television. It received a "62" rating and a "78" share. This translated into a viewing audience of 137 million people.